THE ALHAMBRA

by Desmond Stewart

and the Editors
of the Newsweek Book Division

NEWSWEEK, New York

NEWSWEEK BOOK DIVISION

JOSEPH L. GARDNER   *Editor*

Janet Czarnetzki   *Art Director*

Jonathan Bartlett   *Associate Editor*
Laurie P. Winfrey   *Picture Editor*
Kathleen Berger   *Copy Editor*

S. ARTHUR DEMBNER   *Publisher*

WONDERS OF MAN

MILTON GENDEL   *Consulting Editor*

Mary Ann Joulwan   *Designer, The Alhambra*

Endpapers:
*An intricate design in carved and
painted wood, the ceiling of the
Hall of the Blessing is typical of the
Alhambra's rich embellishment.*

Title page:
*The dressing room of the Royal
Baths contains an alcove where
bathers could relax on mattresses
after their ablutions. The stress
on bathing in Islam stems from
the Koran's making cleanliness
a precondition of worship.*

Opposite:
*The four-foot-high Alhambra Vase
is considered among the finest
examples of the glazed lusterware
pottery for which Nasrid Granada
was renowned.*

ISBN: Clothbound Edition 0–88225–087–6
ISBN: Deluxe Edition 0–88225–088–4
Library of Congress Catalog Card No. 73–87152
© 1974 — Arnoldo Mondadori Editore, S.p.A.
All rights reserved. Printed and bound in Italy.

Contents

Introduction

The Alhambra was the last bastion of the eight-hundred-year Islamic presence in Europe's westernmost extremity, Iberia. It is also the finest example of the architectural style that evolved there, with elements blending delicacy and grace into such perfection that they seem to float, as if disembodied, in the vivid air.

Built during the ebb tide of Spain's Muslim period, the Alhambra seems somehow to encapsulate the entire epoch. Implicit within its walls are the bold advance of the eighth-century warriors who first claimed Iberia for Islam, the glories of the tenth-century Cordoban caliphate, and the tragic turbulence of the long reconquest. A telling reminder of the reconquest is the fortress aspect of the Alhambra, so prominent in the picture at left. But inside the walls, the martial aura of the monument totally disappears. The interior is a veritable fairyland, with evanescent vistas of sky and water, soaring arches fantastically embellished, and halls — whether vast or intimate — whose rampant decor ranges from floral to abstract and includes a running rubric of stately Arabic epigraphy.

Once in Christian hands, the Alhambra fell into disrepair until such nineteenth-century enthusiasts as Washington Irving, Victor Hugo, and Théophile Gautier aroused interest in its romantic past and a concern for its preservation. Thanks in part to them, it is now a Spanish national monument and a tourist attraction of the utmost magnetism. Considerably restored, the Alhambra provides the contemporary viewer with an opportunity to come into contact — at however great a remove — with a culture that for a time provided a brilliant light to a world otherwise largely groping in darkness.

THE EDITORS

ISLAMIC SPAIN
IN HISTORY

I

The Red Citadel

The Iberian Peninsula, shared unequally by Spain and Portugal, projects as a square-shaped pendant from Western Europe. Walled to the north by the Pyrenees, washed by an ocean and a sea, the peninsula encases Europe's major plateau, hot in summer and in winter bleak. But in the south, a flattened triangle is attached to the rough square, its point toward Africa. This triangular province, furthermore, is often described as African because of its warm climate and because of the shrubs and plants that it shares with the torrid continent across the straits. Like Africa itself, the province is far from monotonous. The semitropical conditions along the coast contrast with the Alpine rigors of a snow-capped range — the Sierra Nevada — running parallel to the coast and surging to peaks of over eleven thousand feet. One valley to the northwest of this range contains the richest soil in Spain. Systematically irrigated for at least twelve centuries, the *vega* is green in spring with wheat, barley, and vines, its fields and hillsides thick with citrus and mulberries.

The dominant city of the region containing this verdant plain — whose scattered villas were compared by an Arab poet to "Oriental pearls in an emerald setting" — is Granada. Most derive its name from the pomegranate whose foliage is russet in spring, whose fruit form crimson grenades at the end of summer. Others derive it from a compound supposedly meaning "hill of strangers." What is certain is that, from the early eighth century to the late fifteenth, Granada was no stranger to Muslim immigration from Africa. And here, on a thirty-five-acre plateau atop a last spur of the Sierra Nevada, Spanish Islam produced its last royal palace, the Alhambra.

Twenty sultans of one royal house — it was known as Nasrid, after Nasr the grandfather of its founder — for two and a half centuries enjoyed this majestic residence, which is not only the last but, because it was never taken by assault, the best-preserved monument of a long-lived culture. And although it was achieved at the ebb tide of this culture — when the Muslims ruled only a tiny peripheral kingdom, and that as vassals of the advancing Christians to the north — it is a place of perfection, not fragments, suggesting spiritual balance, not decay. It recalls, perhaps, those great artists — Goethe in words, Monteverdi in music, Titian or Picasso in paint — who have produced great works as they have grown old. The last work may differ subtly from what went before; it may contain premonitions of demise; but as the work of a creative spirit it can blend in triumphant summation the themes of a lifetime. The Alhambra shows in its structures and decoration the aptitudes and tastes, the likes and dislikes, of a civilization whose Eastern traces are India's Taj Mahal and the mosques of Samarkand.

The view of the Alhambra from outside is impressive but not unique. It is not the impression that the modern visitor will most remember. The plain, walled enceinte will look familiar, for the dynasty previous to the Nasrids, the Almohades, had built numerous such strongpoints to defend their embattled faith. But the massive plainness of the Alhambra's exterior has an older ancestry in the East — Christian as well as Islamic. The Byzantines, mindful of Christ's words about the whited sepulcher, all glory without and filth within, had given their great brick churches exteriors as stark and bare as silos, but concealing a veritable

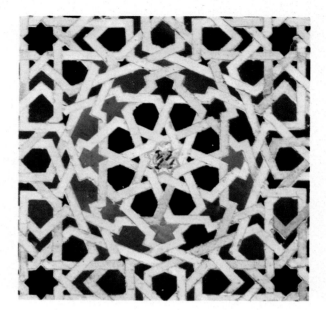

paradise of mosaic and marble inside. This style became general throughout the Middle East.

From Persia and Baghdad in the east to Granada in the west, ordinary people, no less than rulers, built their houses with plain façades. They still do, for this Eastern style conforms with the deepest spirit of Islam. Just as the Muslim woman traditionally reserves her charms for her husband, cumbrously concealing her body and even her face in shapeless cloth, so the Eastern house customarily turns a plain, windowless face to the dusty lane or noisy bazaar. Outside there is nothing to arouse envy — no ornaments to be stolen or defaced. A massive studded door marks the one legitimate break in the unornamented wall. Inside are delights, if the owner is rich, or if not, simple comfort. The delights, the comforts, are reserved for those within, above all for those who come as guests, for Islam outdoes all other cultures in its concern for hospitality. And since Islam has a desert origin, it is useful to remember, in approaching the Alhambra, the contrast between the perilous desert and the oasis, where even an enemy may stay three days without fear.

Just as the desert can glow to beauty in moonlight or at dawn, so the changing light of day gives the bare walls of the Alhambra changing shades of red. The walls owe their redness to bricks made from a ferrous mud. A primitive fort dating from the ninth century was known as *al-Qal'ah al-Hamra*, "the Red Citadel," presumably from being made of these bricks. When in 1238 the first Nasrid ruler urged on the building of his fortress palace, the walls of the rising edifice glowed crimson in the light of the torches. The name was fixed forever and remains today.

The Alhambra occupies a natural acropolis. On its northern side there is a sheer fall of rock to the Darro River, a subtributary of the Guadalquiver. The gorge was an impregnable defense. The towers that punctuate the northern walls conceal habitations, not entrances. On the southern side, toward the plain, were the guarded entrances in the massive walls.

The visitor today, like the American writer Washington Irving nearly a century and a half ago, enters by the massive Gate of Justice. This southern entry is approached by a long road ascending through lofty elms, planted by the Duke of Wellington in his war against Napoleon and joined by chestnuts and other shady trees. A large open hand is sculpted in the keystone of the horseshoe-shaped entry arch. This symbolizes the five requirements of the Islamic faith: belief in the oneness of God, prayer, fasting in the month of Ramadan, pilgrimage to Mecca, and the giving of alms. It underscores the primary function of every Muslim sultan, which was the upholding of the law of Islam. He ruled, at least in theory, according to the system of the laws of God as revealed in the Koran and expounded by jurists, not according to his own impulses or the votes of his subjects.

From the arch — a useful reminder of the religious basis of Islamic power — the visitor passes into a great esplanade now known as the Place of the Cisterns. Although the plateau had its own aqueduct, there was always the danger of besieging enemies cutting off the water, so rain was stored, as it was elsewhere in the Mediterranean, in great chambers cut from the rock. The visitor anxious to understand this Islamic palace need not bother here in the vast esplanade with what

The massive ramparts and stark watchtowers of the Alcazaba, the fortress proper and oldest portion of the Alhambra, serve notice that for all the grace and delicacy within, the Red Citadel was first and foremost a military structure.

Overleaf:
From its virtually impregnable position high above the city, the Alhambra fortress and its outbuildings command a strategic view of Granada and the plain beyond. In the midst of the Alhambra complex can be seen the circle-in-a-square Renaissance Palace of Charles V intruding itself between the Nasrid palace (to its right) and the Alcazaba beyond. Begun in 1524, the incongruous structure was never completed.

will later be his chief annoyance — his camera-slung fellows. Things have changed since Washington Irving had the place to himself except for an invalid soldier mounting guard and a group of others sleeping in their tattered cloaks. In the Place of the Cisterns the wise visitor averts his gaze from the square Renaissance palace of Charles V. It belongs to the centuries that followed the last Nasrid king and to a different order of taste from the building it was designed to eclipse. It is as much an intruder as a giant Buddha would be in the forecourt of Notre Dame; it overlies the Alhambra like an elephant lying on a gazelle.

From this open space a simple portal leads into the Alhambra. "The transition was almost magical," Irving wrote in 1832. "It seemed as if we were at once transported into other times and another realm, and were treading the scenes of Arabian story." The "otherness" that Irving observed in the Alhambra applies less to time and realm — for most of the palaces we visit belong to past times and different countries — than to purpose, structure, and decoration.

The standard European palace derives its name from one of the seven hills in ancient Rome. Augustus, the first Caesar to be worshiped in his lifetime, built his imperial residence on the Palatium, or Palatine Hill. His successors covered the hill with palaces of their own. Caesarian architecture derived its basic style from Greece, but was made more imposing and pompous by the deification of those it housed. The European palace, whether immense like Versailles or modest like Portugal's Queluz, has maintained a tradition in which an imposing structure built in obedience to the laws of symmetry housed incumbents who kept up (until

they were replaced by caretakers) the aura of Caesars. The palace was the grandiose shell in which a charismatic mollusk embodied the state. Hitler's Berlin Chancellery was the debased, and we may well hope final, expression of this idea.

The palatial style and name alike are alien to orthodox Islam. When the British imposed a European-style monarchy on twentieth-century Iraq, an Arabic word derived from Palatium — *bilat* — was used for the royal family's administrative palace. In Islam the two words traditionally used for a ruler's headquarters were *qasr*, "castle," or *qal'ah*, "citadel." These two words conveyed both the practicality and the impermanence of a military installation. The Alhambra, whose defensive site was its prime advantage, combined the equivalent of government offices with the residence of a ruler, or sultan. As a palace, it was not expected to survive intact.

The Islamic buildings that are constructed to survive are mosques (often including tombs) and schools. Palaces were cannibalized or destroyed, for the palace was the headquarters of a man temporarily authorized to enforce the laws of Islam. If a palace also embodied weird fantasy or brilliant daydream, it was as impermanent as these. The ruler's successors would consciously efface or greedily devour what he had left. In Cairo, for example, succeeding dynasts allowed the palaces of their predecessors to crumble into ruins. They constructed new structures to the north, in the direction from which the dominant wind blew, so that the stench of the past would not disturb them. Cairo is flat, so this process was easy.

The Alhambra occupied a restricted and admirably defensible site. It would have been insane for an em-

The Court of the Myrtles (right) with its serene fountain and pool formed the reception area for visitors to the Hall of the Ambassadors. Before reaching that sanctuary, they passed through an antechamber, the Hall of the Blessing, sometimes called Hall of the Boat, apparently due to a confusion between the Arabic baraka ("blessing, benediction") and the Spanish barca ("boat"). The rosette in the lower part of the wall decoration (detail at left) shows the shield of ibn-al-Ahmar, the Alhambra's founder.

battled dynasty to move. Instead, successive Nasrids worked it over. The Alhambra is thus not the work of one founder, but a royal citadel reworked, in the same style, by successive dynasts. That it seems all of a piece is due to the conservative tastes of a dynasty that knew itself threatened and that in its last century was too poor to afford rebuilding. That the Alhambra has survived, unlike the Baghdad palace of Harun al-Rashid or the palace-city of Cairo's Fatimids, is due to its having been surrendered intact to Christian Europeans and maintained by them, first as a trophy and now as a museum.

The Alhambra's atmosphere engenders legends, one of which claims that the building is maintained by magic. When we probe its component materials we may almost believe this, for no building of comparable beauty and durability can have been put together of such flimsy materials. Bricks, wood (often sloppily carpentered behind its decorative shell), and stucco: to these physical ingredients must be added glimpses of sky, beds of myrtle, and especially water, of all elements both the weakest and most potent.

The ground plan of the Alhambra (see diagram, page 165) shows further contrasts with the palaces of Europe. A trip on roller skates through the vast sequences of Versailles, Vienna's Schoenbrunn, or Naples's Caserta would quickly establish affinities as close as those that bound European royalty into one interrelated tribe. The Alhambra, a rectangular jigsaw of patios and rooms, lacks the defined axes of the palaces of the north. The builders had neither the space nor the taste for great formal gardens, such as those that confront Versailles. Even the small gardens that are

there now, like the greenery on the outside, were planted after the Alhambra changed hands. This is because the men who built the Alhambra enjoyed nature in other ways — in the vistas of plain and city from embrasured windows, in the intrusion of water and verdure in one patio, of water and sky in another. Or they enjoyed it in garden palaces, built for summer, of which only the Generalife survives.

If classical schemes were lacking, function nevertheless divided the Alhambra into three sections, though these were interlocked. The first, which the visitor enters from the esplanade, was devoted to justice and administration. The Nasrid sultans were available to their people on Mondays and Thursdays, in the morning. After a recitation from the Koran the citizens would put their pleas before the ruler or his vizier, just as in ancient Arabia the barefoot tribesman had approached his sheikh. This public area has suffered more than any other quarter from depredations. It was until recently a Christian church and the fountain in its patio is new.

Adjoining this area was the second portion of the palace, the Serai. This was the sultan's official residence, where he was at home to more distinguished visitors. Its focus, the Court of the Myrtles, perfectly conveys an essential of Nasrid architecture — its involvement with nature. A central pool reflects colonnades that seem too slender to uphold their weight of decoration and the red brick of the roofs, while the dark green bushes contrast with the gleaming white marble of the paving. The courtyard leads to the loftiest tower in the Alhambra, the Comares Tower. Its bare masonry, nearly 150 feet in height, is broken only by two layers

of windows. These light the Hall of the Ambassadors, where, seated on his throne, the sultan would receive envoys. This function was as vital to Granada as it was to its contemporary, Constantinople, since diplomacy, rather than warfare, was a major weapon used to keep aggressive neighbors at bay. The superb decoration in the hall (to which the visitor returns after he has grasped the structure of the whole) is among the best in the palace.

Linked to the Serai, where the ruler lived his public life, attended only by men, was the third section, the harem. Here he lived his private life as a family man. The word "harem" has undergone semantic degradation in the West, having acquired suggestions of orgiastic debauch. In Arabic the word was linked to the conception of the sacred, or the taboo. The harem symbolized the domestic discretion in which the Muslim, great or small, was supposed to live. The semantic decline is not entirely due to Europe. While the Prophet Muhammad had restricted to four the number of wives a follower could marry, two loopholes made it possible for the wealthy or powerful to enjoy the favors of regiments of women. In the first case, divorce was easy for men, so that, as in the case of Saudi Arabia's first king, Abdul-Aziz ibn-Saud, literally scores of women could be married, often for tribal rather than erotic motives, and then honorably divorced after one night. In the second case, the Muslim was also allowed concubines, whose children were regarded as legitimate.

Some Islamic rulers, including earlier emirs or caliphs in Spain, maintained harems that would dwarf a woman's college. But by the time of the Nasrids, both the means of the state and its customs had changed.

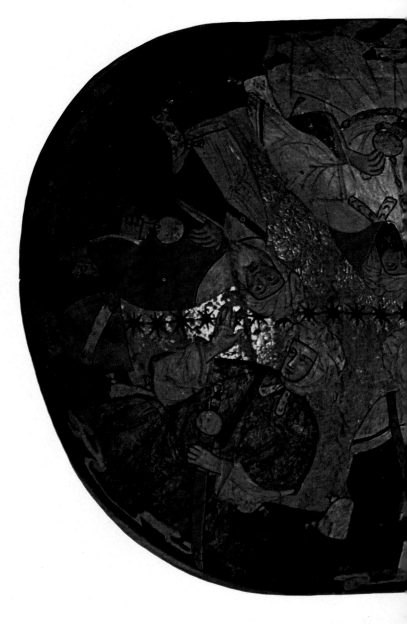

The ceiling shown below was probably painted by a Christian artist — albeit under Muslim auspices — sometime in the late fourteenth century. The room it adorns has come to be called the Hall of the Kings, as the individuals portrayed are traditionally described as representing the first ten Nasrid rulers.

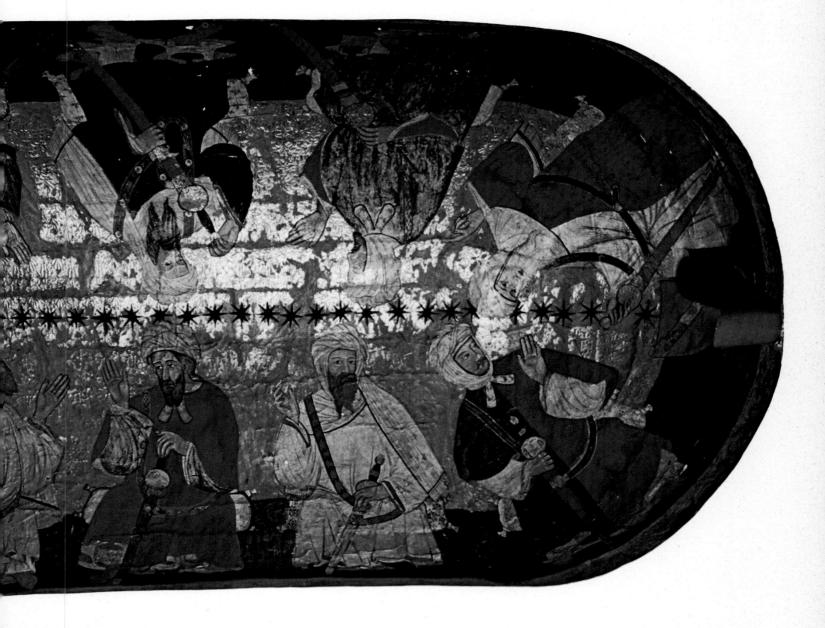

The Christians had reduced the Nasrid monarchy to the area between Granada, Tarifa, and Malaga. At the same time, Muslim manners had been affected by Christianity as much as most Spanish Christians had been affected by Islam. The harem of the Alhambra can never have rivaled the harems of Cordoba or Baghdad, though it must have been larger than what remains today. Its equivalent of a drawing room was the Court of the Lions, while its domestic character is suggested by the surviving baths.

In the spirit that pervades the interlocking sections of the Alhambra there is a persistent aroma of ancient Arabia. Habits deriving from Mecca and Medina influence the structure, while the interweaving of Arabian likes and Arabian prejudices creates the distinctive magic of the style.

In pre-Islamic Arabia, outside the few cities, the usual dwelling was a tent. "Halt, let us weep," begins a still-remembered ode written before the Prophet's revelation, "for remembrance of a loved one and a dwelling." The beloved was a Bedouin girl, the lover a desert prince, and the dwelling a "house of hair." While the short-lived vegetation was green (the product of some capricious storm), while the surrounding sands were still unfouled by their transient visitors (whose camel herds were their wealth and life), the tents offered shade and relaxation. The chief enjoyment of these primitive yet not uncultured people was the recitation of a complex, imagistic poetry, the one art that was, with the Arabs, already developed to sophisticated pitch when they set out on their odyssey through time. The greenery would die, the site would lose its virginal appeal. Overnight the tents would be folded and the sand of the wilderness would efface the desert idyll. So for all its splendor — the product of six centuries in which the Arabs had lived among the peoples of the Mediterranean — the Alhambra can be seen as a mixture of tenting (fantastically embellished), with tent poles or date palms (transformed into slim, upleaping columns surmounted with marvelously varied capitals), and the element most cherished in a thirsty country — water.

Water had been the primary desideratum when the first Nasrid prepared the plateau and equipped it with an aqueduct. Water remains as essential an element in this monument as brick or marble. This love of water, going back to the sparse, palm-set pools of the Arabian deserts, is a curious link with the twentieth-century architecture of Frank Lloyd Wright, so that the Alhambra seems more modern, as well as more ancient, than the European palace. Intimate where Versailles is imposing, more the work of magic and artifice than engineering, the Alhambra speaks of a dynasty whose founder had simple tastes. The roots go deeper still. While the European palace goes back, through an egocentric Bourbon, to a pagan Caesar, the Alhambra goes back to the Prophet Muhammad. When ruling the first Islamic state from Medina, the Prophet lived in what we should consider a hut rather than a house and darned his own clothes. When he died he was buried in total simplicity beneath the earth floor.

To Arabia and its Prophet the Alhambra owes what is, after its blend of masonry with nature, its most distinctive attribute — its decoration.

When from the Court of the Lions we enter what is perhaps the loveliest room in the palace — the Hall of

*The Court of the Lions (above) is open and airy
and has as its focus the famous Lion Fountain,
supported by twelve roughly carved beasts spurting
water from their mouths. To the Islamic architect,
a closed-in garden of this sort, enlivened with
running water and planted with verdant shrubbery
and aromatic herbs, is a symbol of paradise, which
is described in the Koran as "gardens underneath
which rivers flow." As if to underscore this
paradisical aspect, the builders took plain wood and
tile and stucco and from these rude materials
created archways and ornaments that are
masterpieces of variegated beauty (right).*

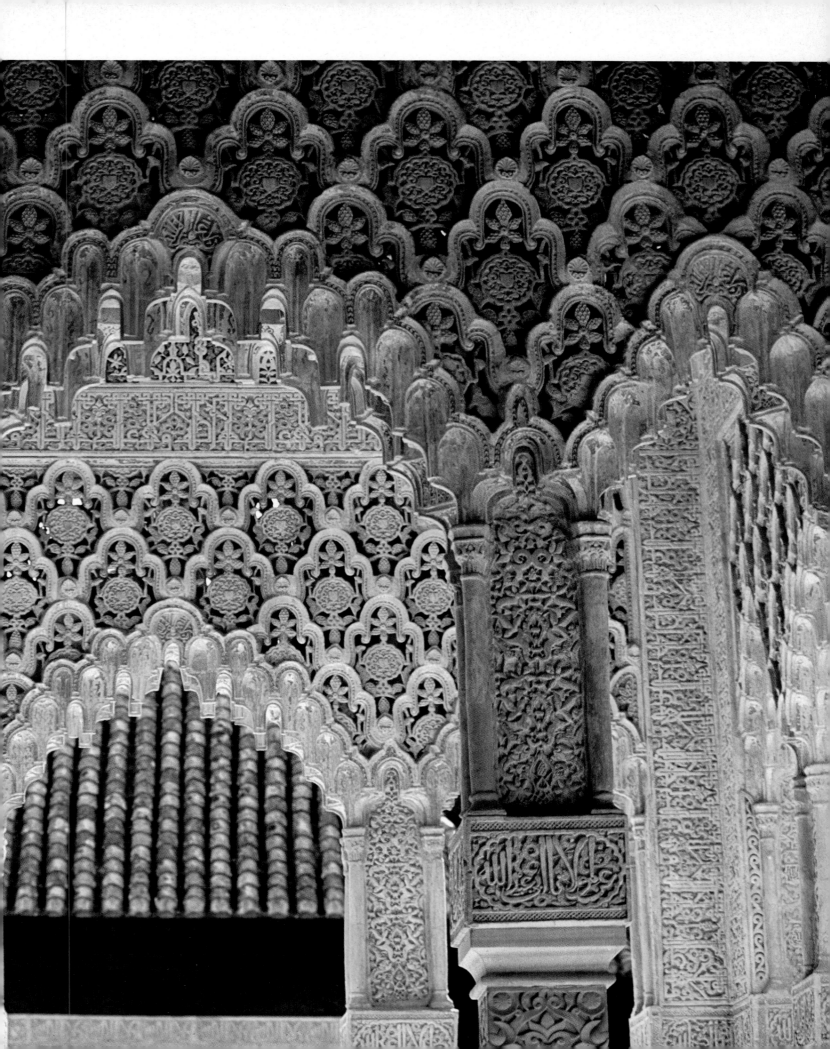

the Two Sisters, with its adjoining mirador — the link may seem tenuous. Nothing in dusty Mecca or palm-set Medina can have resembled this exquisite chamber which takes its name, not from two human sisters, but from twin slabs of flawless white marble laid in the pavement. We see the room emptied of furniture and with some of its inscriptions effaced. But even though the Islamic taste in furniture was almost as austere as that of the Japanese, the room would have contained lamps, glass, carved wood, and worked ivory when the sultan and his companions reclined on the perishable but exquisite stuffs for which their Spain was famous. Verses lining the walls expatiate on the beauties:

> See this wondrous cupola, at whose sight other
>   domes grow pale and vanish:
> The Twins in the sky salute it, to join it the full
>   moon would her place relinquish.

The room has a stalactite ceiling that is without equal. "Nothing can exceed the glory of the honeycomb vaultings," wrote Albert Calvert, an Edwardian enthusiast, "with thousands of fantastic cell formations, each one differing from the other, yet all combining in uniformity. The effect is as if the architect had been assisted in his work by swarms of Brobdingnagian bees."

Yet the link with Arabia, weak though it may be, is real. The decoration of the Alhambra winds back to modes established by the Prophet, or inferred from him. When European palaces had additions made to them, these were at once evident and datable. A classical wing added to a Tudor residence stood out as a new fashion. The frequent additions to the Alhambra — the Gate of Justice and the Court of the Lions both date from the fourteenth century — have the anonymity that has characterized Islam since Muhammad led the pilgrimage to Mecca wearing the same two lengths of white cloth that humbler pilgrims wore. And although no verse in the Koran explicitly condemns representational art, the nation of Muhammad, like the Jews before, generally accepted the inadmissibility of representing men or animals lest such representations might serve as idols, or that with them the artist was in some way trying to rival God, the only giver of life. This negative attitude failed to stifle the exuberant impulses of Islamic artists. Far from abandoning art, they turned their energies in directions strikingly different from those followed in Europe. The Nasrid artists embellished the Alhambra in three basic ways: the carving of stylized foliage; the use of tiles to form elaborate geometric figures in primary colors; and the repetitive use of Arabic calligraphy.

So abstract are these modes of decoration, so impersonal, that the dating of different sections has been a major conundrum to scholars. To the visitor, the problem is almost without importance, as each part of the Alhambra (excluding, of course, the Christian additions) resembles another as much as one spray of honeysuckle resembles the next. The founder of the Nasrids, Muhammad ibn-al-Ahmar, has put the equivalent of his signature on much of the building, however. His motto, omnipresent in the palace, has the sad irony of a man who accepted quasi-sovereignty at the cost of aiding his lord against fellow Muslims in Seville:

This, as written from right to left, reads: *Wa la ghalib ila Allah!* "There is no conqueror but God!"

The convolution of foliage in stucco was one of the innovations made when Islam first came into its own in Iraq and Egypt. The earliest mosques had sometimes been converted churches or parts of churches; if not, they were either buildings erected for Muslims by Christian architects or simple quadrangles with, at one end, pillars supporting an area of shade. In Ahmed ibn-Tulun's great mosque in Cairo, the architects solved the problem in a new way — they encased brick piers with stucco which they then worked. They also used stucco grilles for the windows, which were composed mainly of intricately interlocking circles and segments of circles, each one having a different pattern from the next. Ahmed ibn-Tulun reigned in the ninth century; the stucco work at the Alhambra is the development on different spheres but by the same culture of his innovation.

The geometric ornamentation undoubtedly appealed to an affinity between Islam and mathematics. Some critics have complained of monotony, of repetition, qualities also to be found in Arabic poetry and music. And a quick, crowded tour is more unfair to this kind of beauty than it is to statues, whose tactile impact can flare a message to the emotions, or paintings, which tell a story or show a known face. The geometrical decorations of the Alhambra are visible mantras. They need the kind of absorption we give to wallpaper when lying in bed sick, or the enthralled concentration that comes with the use of hallucinogenic drugs. At the very least we need a cushion, a waterpipe, and silence. We need to be alone with each wall for one morning. Since this is impossible, we may learn more from a book of photographs in our bedroom than from an on-the-

spot visit, which may bewilder to the point of anger.

The third form of decoration — the covering of space with intricately elaborated writing — is both a triumph and a tragedy. The triumph consists in the skill, unsurpassed in any other civilization, whereby artists used the letters of a language to form patterns that delight even the uncomprehending eye. The tragedy is linked closely to the triumph. Because of the reverence paid to the language of the Koran, its users progressively tended to forget the true function of speech — as a means of communicating human needs and ideas and to use it as rhetoric, sporific, or as here, decoration. One of the most pithy and expressive poetic systems devised by man had become, by the time the Court of the Lions was completed, the vehicle for little more than compliments to the powerful or for the reworking of commonplace ideas. The religious texts in the Alhambra (like the motto already quoted of Muhammad ibn-al-Ahmar) are majestic. But the poetry that is inscribed around the basin of the lion fountain lacks the rude vigor of the lions that support it. It has the freshness of a jeweler's shop:

Behold this mass of glistening pearl,
falling within a ring of frothing silver,
to flow amidst translucent gems
than marble whiter, than alabaster more translucent.

The lettering gives the tone of sadness to a building whose perfection proclaims a melancholy truth, symbolized by the hill to the south from which the last Nasrid king, moving into years of exile, sighed his last sigh at the sight of the Alhambra: beauty, itself perishable, outlasts man; man's enjoyment of beauty depends on the caprice of fate and lasts but a moment.

29

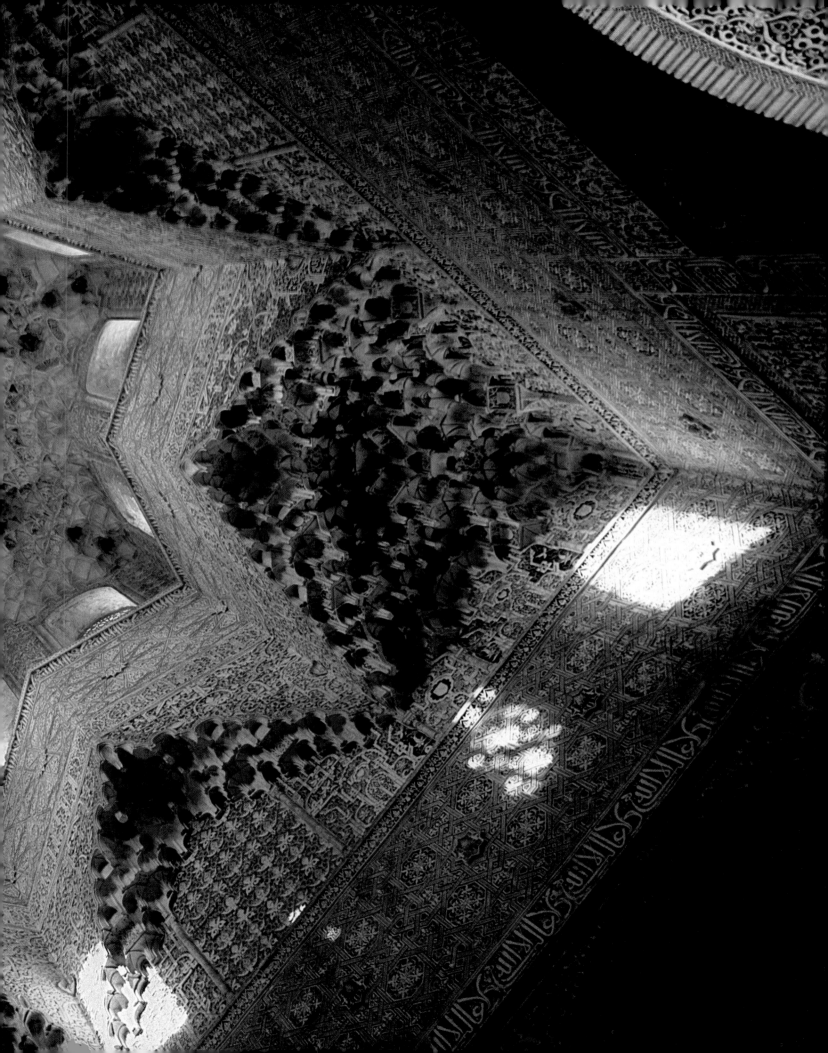

II

Islam's Western Fortress

Not the least of the surprises that the Alhambra offers is that of finding it where it is, in southern Europe. The Renaissance palace added by Charles V has the dubious merit of emphasizing the surprise, for its ponderous façade belongs, however remotely, to Roman Hispania, whose two provinces produced such emperors as Trajan and such writers as Seneca, Lucan, and Martial. The Alhambra, on the other hand, belongs to a culture whose epicenter lay in Arabia and whose creative fallout drifted as far afield as Malacca, Bukhara, and Timbuktu. What miracle transposed these slender, un-Roman columns, these square yards of convoluted and unintelligible epigraphy here? What further miracle allowed this Eastern culture to last, not one generation, but in the south, in Granada, nearly thirty — or a longer period of time than separates Richard Coeur de Lion from Richard Nixon?

Like most miracles, the creation of a Semitic civilization in Spain can be explained in rational terms, though when the explaining has been done, a sense of the miraculous may well creep back.

The Iberian Peninsula had been subject to influences from the eastern Mediterranean long before the arrival of the Arabs. From around 1100 B.C., the Phoenicians had traded with Spain. This remarkable Semitic people from what is now Lebanon founded Gades (the modern Cadiz), which has been called the oldest town in Europe to maintain continuity of life and name. Carthage, itself a colony of Phoenicia, carried Phoenician influence further in the period immediately preceding the rise of Roman power. Cartagena — "New Carthage" — was a Carthaginian fortress commanding the best harbor in southeast Spain, and when Carthage made its supreme

bid to destroy the Roman menace, Hannibal led not only his elephants, but an army with many Spanish soldiers across this land bridge to northern Italy.

As the second Semitic influence to affect Iberia, Arabic-speaking Islam exerted the more intense, more durable hold, because it comprised in a potent trinity a religion, a state, and a culture.

As a religion Islam had burst into the Mediterranean world in the first half of the seventh century, while at the same time reaching deep into central Asia and even India. Muhammad ibn-Abdullah, a young Meccan of good family but reduced circumstances, endowed with a pleasing manner and possessed of a reliability that won him the nickname of al-Amin ("the Faithful"), attracted the attention of a woman merchant fifteen years his senior. She chose him first to be her agent and then her husband. She proved his first convert when, around A.D. 610, he had the first of a series of audile revelations which convinced him that he was the last prophet of the One God in a chain going back through Jesus and Moses to Abraham, the father, through Ishmael, of the Arab people. These revelations, which continued throughout his life, were codified shortly after Muhammad's death in 632. Forming a book of roughly New Testament length, they are known in Arabic as *al-Qur'an al-Karim,* "The Noble Recitation."

It is important, in order to understand the swiftness with which Muhammad's message created an empire of new believers, to note that he did not claim to be initiating a new religion. And in claiming instead that Islam ("Submission to God") was a restatement of the traditional monotheism of the Middle East, he posed a striking and at the same time insidious challenge to

the Christian churches of the Mediterranean, and in particular to those under Byzantine rule.

By the time of Muhammad's birth, the simple and electrifying gospel of Jesus of Nazareth had passed from a phase of persecution to a state of triumph. From a new Rome, named Constantinople in his honor, Constantine, a baptized Caesar, ruled an empire formally set under the authority of Christ. The simple camaraderie of the catacombs was dissolved by success and while the new society based on love might still be found in some homes and some monasteries, Constantine's acceptance of Christianity brought about traumatic changes. The Caesars who accepted Christ were no less cruel than the Caesars who had worshiped Jupiter. The tax collectors who collected for the New Rome used torture as briskly as those who had come before. Institutions such as slavery continued. The skills of the persecutor were now employed against the Jews — for not accepting Jesus as the Messiah — as well as against heretics, and heretics became more numerous as the doctrines of the Church became increasingly more complex and difficult to understand.

Disillusionment with official Christianity (but not with Jesus himself) was particularly bitter in such regions of the Byzantine empire as Egypt and North Africa, where Greek-speaking Christians dominated non-Europeans. Many of the heresies that flourished in North Africa (where the Greek epithet "barbarian" was applied so persistently that it has stuck as "Berber") represented assertions of identity by oppressed groups as much as genuine devotion to doctrinal minutiae. So the ease with which Egypt and North Africa fell to Islam between 640 and 705 can largely be explained by the resentment of native populations to Byzantine misrule. The Berbers and the Egyptian Christians, or Copts, saw in the new religion a simpler variant of what they believed already, coupled with the inestimable advantage of an easier tax system.

Arabic Islam, contrary to what has often been said of it, was far from being a bigoted or fanatical religion. The Arabians who had produced in Muhammad a religious genius were not themselves theologically minded. Pleasure-loving — their major delights being poetry, genealogy, and horsemanship — they had compelling material reasons for not trying too hard to convert all of their new subjects. The Koran ordained that monotheists, such as Jews and Christians, should be given a choice of becoming Muslims or remaining as they were, subject to paying a head tax. But this head tax, which was not levied on women, children, or the old, was less onerous than the Byzantine imposts, and thus pleasing to the taxed. To the Arabs, who enjoyed fighting, this source of revenue represented the means whereby they could constitute a standing army, ever ready to push forward the frontiers of their faith and to increase their plunder. During the first century after the death of the Prophet's immediate followers this army was controlled by the Beni Umayya, or Umayyad dynasty, who as proud Arabs preferred to keep the administered populations of their new empire as tax-paying *dhimmis,* or protected non-Muslim minorities.

In bringing Islam to the Berbers — who stretched from the western oases of Egypt to the Atlantic — the Arab generals released the energies of this sturdy and admirable people who till then had scarcely been allowed to show their talents on the stage of history.

It would be a mistake to see the conquest and Islamization of the Berbers in too hasty a perspective. At first Arab tribal pride antagonized the proud Berber mountaineers, involving the first century of Islam in revolts, massacres, and reconquests. But in the long term the Berbers were transformed into devoted Muslims, as ready for fighting as the Arabs and perhaps more sincerely interested in the religion that was its justification. As early as 670, the Arabs had established a military capital for North Africa at Qairwan in modern Tunisia; by 705, the whole northern area of the Dark Continent was consolidated under Islamic power.

In the spring of 711, a largely Berber force of some seven thousand men landed in southern Spain. They had been preceded by a smaller reconnoitering force the previous year. Their leader was Tariq ibn-Ziyad, a Berber client of Musa ibn-Nusayr, the Arab governor of Northwest Africa. Tariq, who was to bequeath his name to Gibraltar — *Jebal Tariq,* "Mountain of Tariq" — landed in a season when Spain combined the appeals of spring and autumn. The countryside was burgeoning with blossoms, rivaling Damascus, till then the Arabs' symbol of fertility. The country as a whole was as ripe for plunder as an unguarded fruit tree.

After the fifth-century collapse of the Roman Empire in the West, Spain had suffered invasion by two successive waves of barbarian peoples from eastern Europe. The Vandals, who pillaged through the country on their way to found a kingdom in Carthage, left as their legacy little other than two important words: "vandalism," a term for wanton destruction, and "Vandalicia," the origin of Andalucia (in Arabic, *al-Andalus*), the name that the Arabs were to give their Spanish realm.

The Spaniards use the term to this day for their vast southern region.

The second group, the Visigoths, represented a governing class more than a folk migration. A Germanic and tribal aristocracy pushed west by the Huns, they took over — first in Gaul, then in Spain — the ravaged provinces of the Western Roman Empire. Their rule mixed the factious tribalism typical of wandering barbarians with Roman oppression and weighed as heavily on the local people as that of the worst proconsuls. In place of Roman order, however, they inflicted chaos in their territories by their chronic disputes over who should next be elected king. Their regime had only one durable achievement, the establishment of Roman Catholicism as the state religion. Even this achievement, however important for the distant future of Spain, carried the seeds of immediate disaster, for many Christian Spaniards adhered to the Arian doctrine, which put them on the block for heresy, while the Jews, who formed an influential element in every important Spanish town, aroused the zeal of persecutors.

History shows that to be successful in oppression, a regime must be united. The Visigoths had constant jealous schisms. A squabble over the succession to the throne seems to have opened the way to the Muslims, who were invited to cross into Spain — only temporarily, of course — by one party to the dispute. The Muslims accepted the invitation to discover not only a country preserving much of the wealth of Roman times, but a divided populace of overtaxed peasants, embittered heretics, and persecuted Jews, none with any great loyalty to Roderick, their Visigothic king.

Owing to Roderick's absence in the north, Tariq

35

had ample time to establish a base near the modern city of Algeciras. Roderick rushed south only to lose first a battle, in which a disaffected part of his army withdrew from the fighting, and then his life. The Islamic army was then in a position to push past Cordoba (which shortly surrendered) to Toledo, the Visigothic capital, which capitulated without resistance. The following year the Umayyad governor of Qairwan, Musa ibn-Nusayr, joined Tariq on Spanish soil, this time with a largely Arab army of some eighteen thousand. In the course of 712, Musa occupied Seville, and by 714 he was on his way back to Damascus (probably demoted for too great success), having with Tariq conquered virtually the whole of the peninsula. To his son Abd-al-Aziz he left the task of capturing Pamplona at the western end of the Pyrenees and Tarragona and Narbonne on the Mediterranean coast.

Thus within five years of their first tentative landing, the Muslims had destroyed the Visigothic state and replaced it with an administration whose military forces exercised far more effective control. But what the Berbers and Arabs had not done — and never were to do — was to uproot the Spanish population radically. As in other conquered provinces — Iraq and Egypt, for example — the majority of the people living in the territory were those who had lived there before the arrival of Islam; they remained the basic stock to which the Muslims were merely additions.

By the end of the eighth century, Spain supported a racially and religiously mixed society unique in the Europe of the day and rare anywhere at any time. The first wave of Arabs who had entered Spain under Musa ibn-Nusayr were later joined by a second, from Syria, after a Berber revolt had caused the Damascus caliph to send reinforcements to North Africa. The Arabs settled in the lands that were most like those they knew in Syria and were the most easily cultivated: the valley of the "Great River" (in Arabic, *Wadi al-Kebir,* now Guadalquivir), including Seville and Cordoba; and the coastal plain that edged the central plateau from the south all the way up the east coast as far as the fertile valley of the Ebro, including the important city of Saragossa. The Berbers occupied the plateau regions, which in many respects resembled the hilly areas of North Africa where they had raised sheep and tended fruit trees. The Christians, whether of Iberian, Roman, or Visigothic origin, coexisted with the Muslims throughout the peninsula, but in the northwest remained the overwhelming majority.

These divisions were naturally less rigid than they might appear. Arabs lived in such cities as Toledo, within a largely Berber area, and some Berbers lived in such predominantly Arabic cities as Cordoba and Seville. In the Muslim cities the Christians sometimes shared their places of worship with the adherents of the new faith, at least for a time. They were then allowed to build substitute churches in the suburbs. The Jews, who had actively helped the Muslims wrest the country from its Visigothic masters, lived as a protected minority in the chief cities. Their situation was greatly improved by Islamic rule, for, no longer an outcast community, they enjoyed a status similar to that of the Christian majority.

The Pyrenees were not the limits of Muslim incursion into Western Europe. What has often been termed a decisive battle was fought south of Poitiers in France

The cultural legacy of the Visigoths before the Islamic conquest is meager. It does, however, include a few objects of great richness, including jeweled crowns, one of which (right) bears the name of King Recceswinth (who reigned between 653 and 672). The filigree gold of this crown is set off with pearls and sapphires. Only one illuminated manuscript is widely accepted as having its provenance in Visigothic Spain. Known as the Ashburnham Pentateuch, it includes the story of Jacob and Esau (below).

in 732. But Charles Martel's important victory was
symbolic not so much of a tide stemmed as a tide ebb-
ing. There were no Arabs — at this time still the chief
missionaries of Islam — to carry the frontier forward
and to settle the land behind it. Arabia, from whose
overpopulated interior the Arabs had poured, was too
far away, and by this time too emptied, to supply further shock troops for the Prophet. And by the time that
Spain had built up its own considerable Islamic population, the missionary impetus had· gone and the Europeans had recovered from their first alarm.

It will never be possible to calculate precisely the
Arab percentage in the Spanish population, either in
the early or late periods of Islamic rule. But though
numerically only a fraction of even the Muslim population, it was the formative element. Arabic, the language
of the Koran, was the dominant tongue, even though
Romance (as we may term the late-Latin language of
the Spaniards) was also widely spoken at all times.
Berber, on the other hand, put down no roots on
European soil. The unique prestige of the Koran in
part explains the dominance of Arabic. To Muslims
the Koran was the equivalent, not of the New Testament, but of Jesus himself. It stood for divine intervention in human history. Regarded as the uncreated
word of God, existent before time, the Koran had been
conveyed to Muhammad by the angel Gabriel, who
had similarly conveyed to Mary the news of the coming
of Jesus. Because of the sanctity of the Koran, Muslims
conceded to Arabic a prestige which the Arabs, proud
of their language, demanded in any case and which its
development in poetry, and later in prose, further
enhanced. Even many of the Spaniards who never

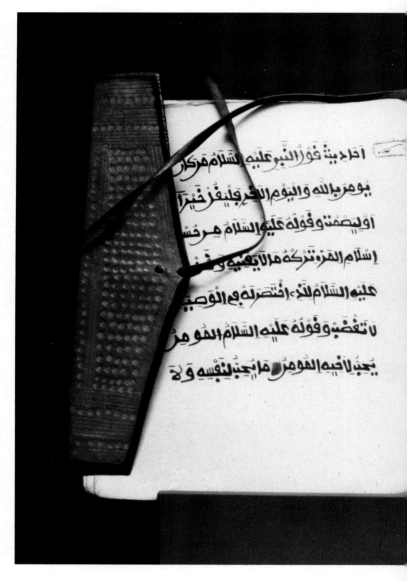

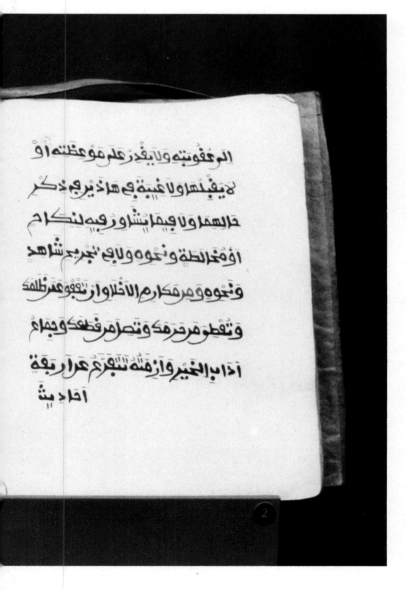

changed their religion became infatuated with the language of the caliphs.

Another factor contributed to the Arabs' prestige. Being — or claiming to be — descended from the Prophet's Companions and Helpers (two separate categories in Islamic history), they formed an aristocracy much in the same manner as the descendants of the Normans who crossed into Saxon England with William the Conqueror. Their own pride of race made the Arabs more than willing to assume this aristocratic role, but as their traditions and laws permitted them to marry foreign women — a man's descent being traced through his father only — many proud nobles were genetically far from being as Arab as they claimed.

One of history's *coups de theatre* also helped ensure the purity as well as the dominance of Arab influence — so much so that the first three centuries of Islamic rule in Spain were more Arab than Islamic, with the Arab tradition maintained there more resolutely than it was in the Middle East. The Umayyad caliphs, who had moved from Arabia to Damascus, were little affected by either Hellenic or Persian influences and steadfastly maintained their Meccan manners in their new role as empire builders. This made them increasingly unpopular as the empire grew to include more and more Muslims of non-Arab stock. Islam had overthrown the ancient Persian empire of the Iranian plateau even more swiftly and decisively than it overthrew that of the Byzantine, and the Persians had been converted to Islam but were ruled somewhat as second-class citizens.

Being heirs to an ancient and sophisticated civilization, the Persians not only resented such treatment but

The Sacred House of Islam, the Kaaba, is shown above from a fifteenth-century scroll. According to Muslim belief, it marks the site where Ishmael, the legendary father of the Arabs, worshiped, and houses the Black Stone, given to Ishmael by the angel Gabriel.

had the determination and power to do something about it. A rival branch of the Prophet's family, known as Abbasids from their descent from Muhammad's paternal uncle Abbas, headed a movement first of sedition, then of revolt. In 747 an Abbasid general, Abu Muslim, raised the black flag of the new dynasty in Khorasan. By June 750, Damascus had fallen and by August the same year the last Umayyad caliph, Marwan II, had been murdered in Egypt, where he had fled. The new dynasty symbolized a shift of center to the east. Damascus was abandoned for a new capital, Baghdad, in central Iraq. Between eighty and ninety surviving Umayyads were assured that they could live in peace with the new dynasty and were invited to a feast of reconciliation in Damascus. The doors of the banqueting hall were shut, the guests were butchered, and their hosts sat down to enjoy grilled meat and sherbet. The Abbasids had the graves of most Umayyad caliphs desecrated, thinking by so doing to finish with their line forever.

But on the day of the festive killing, the absence of two brothers, grandsons of the Umayyad caliph Hisham who had suspiciously stayed at home, was noticed and soldiers were sent to kill them in their palace. One perished, but the other, Abd-al-Rahman ibn-Muawiyah, was out indulging in the typically Umayyad sport of hunting. He immediately set out on an epic journey west that would seem incredible if told by Hollywood. Escaping further attempts on his life and seeing yet another brother slaughtered by the implacable enemies of his family, he reached first Egypt and then Berber North Africa. This was his obvious escape route, not only because the East was pro-Abbasid, but

because his mother had been a Berber slave girl. Aided only by one faithful servant, he lived for five dangerous years as a hungry fugitive in the Atlas Mountains. But instinct, or calculation, led him steadily west until in 755 he found himself at Ceuta, staring across the Strait of Gibraltar. He saw the southern tip of a country in almost as chaotic a condition as it had been under the Visigothic kings. A chronic rivalry between two main divisions of tribal Arabs put the survival of an Islamic Spain in doubt.

Like Tariq before him, Abd-al-Rahman crossed into Andalus as an ally of one of the warring factions. Between 756, when he won his first decisive battle, and 763, when he defeated the last Abbasid attempts to unseat him, his courage and determination enabled him to transplant his dynasty to Spain and to create there an independent emirate, or kingdom. His surviving Umayyad kinsmen and adherents were encouraged to move west and settle near him. Although the physical unity of Islam was now broken, there remained a spiritual and cultural unity. The customary Friday prayers were still offered in the name of the Abbasid caliph in Baghdad.

Although involved in a blood feud with the Abbasid dynasty, Abd-al-Rahman and his fifteen successors constantly reinvigorated the Arabic element in their state by inviting leading Arabs from the East to settle in their midst. To cite only one example: Abd-al-Rahman's great-grandson, Abd-al-Rahman II, welcomed to Spain Ziryab, the famous musician of the court of Harun al-Rashid. Treated like a prince, surrounded by horsemen and reputedly worth more than thirty thousand gold pieces, Ziryab lived the last thirty-five years

The massive Rock of Gibraltar looms through the mist to beckon travelers from Morocco — just as it did centuries ago. The first Muslim to succumb to the temptation was Tariq ibn-Ziyad. He is said to have been ferried across the strait by a Christian, Count Julian, the exarch of Ceuta, last Byzantine possession in North Africa. Legend asserts that Julian was avenging the violation of his daughter, Florinda, by Roderick, king of the Visigoths. He is further said to have made a raid in the vicinity of Algeciras, where this picture was taken, the year before the Muslim incursion to show how feeble the resistance would be. While it is probable that the count did assist the Muslims, it is likely he did so for booty, the Florinda story being almost certainly pure myth.

of his life in Cordoba. His influence, similar to that of Petronius Arbiter at the court of Nero, was felt in all matters of luxury and taste, not just in music and song. He introduced a liking for glass drinking vessels, instead of gold or silver goblets; he introduced new menus and new styles of dress; he is even credited with having opened an institute of beauty where the use of cosmetics and hairdressing were studied.

A key to the Arab genius was its openness to ideas. Indeed, with their desert background and without this openness, the Arabs could have made no progress. The only art in which they naturally excelled, the Arabs admitted, was poetry. To them, Arabic was the best of all languages and any attempt at translating the Koran seemed blasphemous. Apart from this, their respectful attitude toward older cultures, such as the Greek or Persian, was enforced by a much-quoted Saying of the Prophet: "Seek for knowledge — even in China." The personality of the Arab genius was distinctive enough not to be submerged. It was able to combine elements from many different sources in something that was both new yet recognizably its own.

This synthesizing talent enabled the Arabs to bind together peoples very different from themselves and from one another. In this work of cultural synthesis over a great area they had a notable predecessor in the Roman Empire. Rome had united the peoples who lived around the Mediterranean matrix. The Arabs did something analogous for an empire that for the first time linked half of the Mediterranean with the hitherto isolated culture of Iran. On a smaller scale they showed this same talent in Spain. Andalus was to prove not a country in which alien invaders held

down a resentful populace, but a mixed society in which different groups made their distinctive contributions and finally blended in an original unity.

The Berbers in particular came into their own in Islamic Spain. Their particular qualities were courage in war, hardihood in farming, honesty in personal dealings, and a passionate attachment to saints or holy men. Their fighting qualities proved a major resource in keeping the forces of a rebounding Christendom at bay. The major attempt to reconquer Spain in the lifetime of Abd-al-Rahman I was defeated by other factors, however. In 778, Charlemagne had to recall his army from Spain to meet trouble nearer home; his army's defeat under Roland at Roncesvalles in the Pyrenees was at the hands of Basques, not Muslims, despite the later myth. But during long, unilluminated centuries, it was the Berbers who were the backbone of a defensive system that maintained a kind of no-man's-land between Andalus and Christendom. Three great frontier tracts, known as the Marches, were dotted with castles and small forts. From these, annual sorties would be made into the lands of the infidels; in these, the frontier Muslims would resist the counter raids of the Christians. Life in the Marches was precarious and unpleasant, endurable only by those who were both stolid and brave.

The talents of the native Spaniards had flowered in the silver age of Rome, only to wilt in Roman decay and Visigothic anarchy. The new Pax Islamica enabled the Spaniards, whether they embraced Islam, as many did, or remained Christians, as did many others, to contribute to a culture characterized, for the first time since the fall of Rome, by a proliferation of vigorous and prosperous cities. The Jews, too, made notable contributions to this flourishing urban society as merchants, physicians, and artisans.

The Arabs were able to found their state in southwest Europe thanks to the factions that had sundered the Visigothic ruling class. Ironically, a similar tendency among the ruling Arabs was, in the long run, to produce a political chaos only too tempting to new exploiters. The genius of the Umayyads was manifested in the ability to control, if not heal, these schisms for two and a half centuries. But when at last even their redoubtable line grew weak, their kingdom was to collapse as suddenly as a pantomime castle. Yet the culture that the Umayyad state had protected and to which Islam was the metaphysical impulse continued on, producing its most remarkable fruits first under the warring kinglets who succeeded the Umayyads and then under the invasions of new barbarians from the Sahara and the Atlas Mountains area.

The final destruction of Islam's western forces was to come from the north, not from the south or from within. It has been said with some truth that the Arabs have only flourished in lands where the olive grows. Two oliveless regions — rainswept, Celtic Galicia in the northwest and the mountain bastion of the Asturias in the north — had provided refuge for the small but resolute element in Spain that had never been subdued by the arms or lured by the attractions of the Islamic state. From this untempting and overlooked land emerged the final threat to Spanish Islam. Its eventual achievement would be the eviction of the Jews and Muslims and the capture of the Alhambra and its transformation to its present state as a museum.

III

The Cordoba Caliphate

For longer than the independent existence of the United States — from the middle of the eighth century until the early eleventh — Cordoba ruled the most advanced state in Western Europe. This Spanish city of 200,000 buildings, with Arabic as its official tongue and Mecca as the focus of its rulers' prayers, was the first true metropolis in the West since the fall of Rome. Although the Cordoban empire was never comparable with that of Rome — at its apex it controlled not quite all of Iberia along with part of North Africa — the world of Islam, of which it formed part, comprised a homogeneous society as vast as that of the Romanized Mediterranean. From Spain it stretched across North Africa and by way of Egypt and the Middle East to the confines of China. As in the Roman Empire, ideas and fashions moved with speed from one province to another. Muslims were religious. The magnet of religious pilgrimage drew them to Mecca from all over the world for one overwhelming experience in the hot Arabian sun. They were also inquisitive and acquisitive to a remarkable degree. Journeys prompted by curiosity or the desire of gain also kept them in movement.

The creation of the Cordoban state as Islam's western buttress was the work of the descendants of the fugitive prince, Abd-al-Rahman, who had replanted the Umayyads where the Persian-backed dynasty of the Abbasids could not reach them. Originally an emirate, or kingdom, at its height the Cordoban state claimed to be much more: a caliphate.

Although the Spanish Umayyads represented a constant defiance to the caliphs of Baghdad, pride in their Arab origins inspired them to make of Andalus a realm in which Arab culture remained more vigorous than in the East, where Persian and then Turkish influences were increasingly dominant. Cordoba fostered a society whose harmonious complexities have few parallels; the various layers that made up this society exhibited a way of life such as had not been lived before on Western European soil and has not been lived since.

The apex of this society was formed by the Umayyad ruler and his household. The extraordinary rulers of this dynasty looked different, and lived in a different manner, from their Middle Eastern forebears. The thread of continuity was paternal descent, but because Muslims could freely marry women from other faiths, the family's genetic connection with Arabia had loosened. Even in Syria the Umayyads had sired children by non-Arab women, and the first independent emir of Andalus, Abd-al-Rahman I, himself was the son of a Berber mother. Since intermarriage with Berber, then Frankish, maidens became usual, the typical Spanish Umayyad was tall and ruddy-complexioned with hair that was naturally reddish or even blond. But so strong was the prestige of Arab descent that the Umayyads dyed their hair black to emphasize the prized connection with the Prophet's tribe of Koreish. The changes from ancestral behavior were even stronger.

In Mecca, where the family had originated, the Beni Umayya had been aristocrats, the equivalent on a desert scale of the patrician families of mercantile Venice. In Damascus they had ruled an empire built by the enthusiasm for Islam, fighting, and plunder of three generations of Arabian emigrants. The Umayyads had been first among tribal equals. To their subjects they had been accessible and not particularly awesome,

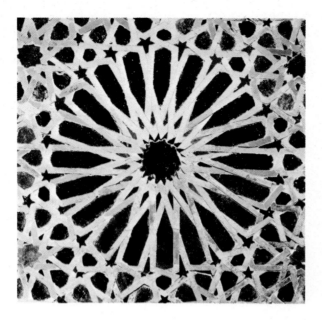

despite their titles of Commander of the Faithful and Caliph. (The word "caliph" derives from an Arabic word meaning successor; the caliphs succeeded Muhammad in his role, not as prophet, but as head of the Islamic community). Desert palaces allowed them to hunt by day and drink by night (the family, although it could boast only one caliph noted for his piety, Omar II, otherwise produced poets of note and at least one formidable debauchee). But the way of life of the Umayyads changed in Cordoba because it had changed elsewhere and because, despite its dynastic schism, Andalus still looked to the Middle East for cultural inspiration.

The Arab mode of rule during this time was evolving in Baghdad under Persian influence. In the Abbasid city west of the Tigris, the dread apparatus of the headsman — a leather mat beside the throne — symbolized the caliph's instantaneous power to draw blood; the prostration required of those received in audience symbolized his godlike remoteness; and while the barracks of foreign praetorian guards represented new sources of power, the grilles of the harem symbolized the ultimate degeneration of the awe-girt rulers.

In Spain, the same process worked itself out. An awe-surrounded autocracy reached its zenith in 929 when Abd-al-Rahman's descendant, Abd-al-Rahman III — the eighth in line — declared himself caliph as well as emir, taking the throne name of al-Nasir li-din-Allah ("Champion of the Religion of God"). One of history's ablest rulers, Abd-al-Rahman III was no megalomaniac. His gesture did not imply a claim to be what he was never within an ocean of being, the ruler of all Muslims. Abd-al-Rahman had not swollen; the title of caliph had shrunk. He was simply claiming to be *a*

caliph, since there were now others in the East and, for him most to the point, another within proximity of Spain. For in 909 a family claiming descent from the Prophet's daughter Fatima had established a Tunisian base from which they were to proclaim themselves rivals to the caliph in Baghdad (later in the century they moved their capital to Cairo). The Fatimid family, or its apologists, claimed that the caliphate was only valid if it went to those who were in the direct line of descent from the Prophet through Fatima's marriage to Ali, the Prophet's cousin and the fourth caliph. (The Umayyads, like the Abbasids, were descended from a collateral branch of the Prophet's family.) Islam had many malcontents for whom the Shiites, or party of Ali, had powerful appeal. The Fatimid claims could thus be dangerous in Spain as elsewhere.

But whatever the motives, the assumption of caliphal titles increased the distance between Abd-al-Rahman III and his subjects. As often happens when men raise themselves higher than their fellows, immediate glory can be a brief stepping-stone to disaster and Umayyad power was to collapse a brief fifty years after the caliph's death. Nonetheless the second half of the tenth century saw Muslim control of the Iberian Peninsula at its most complete, and the caliph's way of life reflected this glory. Its most spectacular manifestation was a new style of palace-city whose remote descendant was to be the Alhambra.

The first Umayyads had lived in the city itself, in a Cordoban palace called "al-Rustafa," after one outside Damascus built by the grandfather of Abd-al-Rahman I. But to fit his new style, and because Cordoba had grown, Abd-al-Rahman III decided to construct a

A ruined courtyard (above) and crumbling outbuilding
(right) are all that remain of the once vast and opulent
palace-city of Abd-al-Rahman III, Medinat al-Zahra.
The caliph named it for the favorite wife who suggested
its construction, and allegedly had a statue of the lady
erected over the main gate.

palace-city three miles to the west of his capital on the lower slopes of the Sierra Morena on a site that, though less defensible than the plateau of the Alhambra, was four times larger. The new complex consisted of three terraces. The upper terrace contained the caliph's reception rooms, residence, and harem. The second terrace contained a botanical garden with shrubs and flowers from all Muslim countries and a small game park. The lowest terrace contained a large mosque and the dwellings of servants and slaves. The palace-city was named Medinat al-Zahra, after the caliph's favorite wife. The work began around 936 and continued for forty years. Abd-al-Rahman (who died before its completion) devoted a third of his vast revenues to erecting this palace and other buildings. According to Arab historians, the palace contained 4,300 pillars and 500 decorated doorways. Those pillars that did not come from the copious Roman ruins in North Africa were imported by sea from Italy, France, and the Byzantine empire, or fashioned new from the quarries of Andalus.

The caliph maintained good relations with the Byzantine emperor in Constantinople as a makeweight against his Islamic rivals, and this Byzantine influence may have contributed to the weakening of the traditional Muslim taboo on artistic representation. Two famous fountains in the palace owed their beauty to the sculptor's art. One, of gilt bronze with bas-reliefs of human figures, had come from Constantinople; the other, of green marble, had come from Syria and was surrounded in its patio by figures of lions, crocodiles, deer, and different species of fowl. These figures, made in Andalus itself, were inlaid with gems and spouted water from their mouths or beaks. The caliph showed himself interested in novel, as well as traditional, manifestations of regal opulence. A century earlier an insomniac Egyptian ruler had used quicksilver to support a floating bed. Abd-al-Rahman used quicksilver — plentiful in Spain — as part of his machinery of ostentation. Around a central pool of this mysterious element were walls and ceilings of marble inlaid with gold; on each side eight doors of ebony and gold were set between further piers of colored marble and crystal. In this hall, the caliph received ambassadors. While he entertained his guests, perhaps displaying the room's chief ornament — a gigantic pearl presented to him by Leo, ruler of the Byzantine empire — he would signal a slave who would then disturb the pool. At once the hall became an inhabited kaleidoscope, coruscating in circular dazzle while the quicksilver continued to lilt.

During a reign of forty-nine years Abd-al-Rahman, it should be stressed, used such devices with deliberation. No slave of pleasure himself, he ruled a wealthy and complex state through carefully chosen ministers, including a *hajib,* or chamberlain, and a series of viziers, or ministers, who had at their disposal an organized police force.

Less functional was the social layer immediately beneath the caliph. The *khassa,* or aristocracy, believed, like other elites, that their innate worth would consolidate their claims forever. The *khassa* consisted preeminently of those related by kinship to the royal household. They included Umayyads who had survived the Abbasid massacre and had filtered west, and the offspring of the emirs and caliphs. Since the first caliph's harem consisted of 6,300 women, these could be numerous. The *khassa,* who were theoretically all

The bronze deer at right once overlooked one of the fountains in the Medinat al-Zahra, a reconstructed room of which appears below. The city, which housed some twelve thousand people, was one of incomparable beauty and richness. It was totally destroyed in 1010 during a revolt by Berbers against the massively incompetent caliph Muhammad II, called "the Winemaker" because he built a winery in the palace during his brief, disastrous tenure.

The craftsmen of Cordoba were famous throughout Europe, and at its height the city boasted thirteen thousand weavers alone. It was not for its woven goods, however, that the city achieved its greatest renown, but for its leathercraft, especially shoes. This speciality is commemorated even today in the English words "cordwainer" — originally a Cordoban — for shoemaker and "cordovan" for a special kind of leather. Cordoban shoemakers were depicted in paintings showing scenes from the life of Saint Mark in a cathedral near Barcelona (left).

descended from the Meccan tribe of the Koreish, received pensions from the royal purse and were organized in a syndicate whose spokesman represented their interests with the ruling sovereign. In general they took no part in public affairs or administration but on major religious occasions, or the reception of ambassadors, they ranked immediately after the ruler and before his ministers and high officials. Members of the *khassa* were sometimes dispossessed if they ran afoul of the ruler, and rich unrelated individuals, including some liberated slaves, could on occasion slip into its paddock.

Below the aristocracy came the Muslim population, whether professional men, merchants, artisans, or peasants. These were either descended from Arab and Berber invaders or more often from Spaniards who from motives of conviction or advantage had accepted the dominant faith. This Muslim population took no part in politics, though its young men could be called upon to fight on the frontiers. A middle-class preoccupation was to reconcile the demands of religion with sensual appetite, which, in the idyllic climate of southern Spain, was not difficult to achieve. Artisans and peasants strove to evade the tax collector. When they could not, and when taxes were onerous, they could give their support to rebels.

Below the Muslim plebs were the Christians and the Jews, on an equal level. The Christians who lived under Islamic rule were generally known as Mozarabs, from an Arabic noun meaning "Arabizers." While remaining inside the fold of Latin Christianity, with a metropolitan at Toledo and many sees, they accepted Islamic culture not only because it was dominant but because it was attractive. Not all Christians made this transition. Priests in particular found themselves socially displaced by the coming of Islam. Whereas under the Visigoths they had formed a privileged caste, under the Arabs they were tolerated but not liked. The distaste was mutual.

"The Arabs," the famous Dutch historian Reinhart Dozy has written, "who combined a refined sensuality with vivacity and good-humour, could not fail to inspire with invincible repugnance priests whose hearts were fixed on estrangement from the world, on abject self-denial and galling penances." The priests knew as little of Muhammad's teaching as most *qadis* (or Islamic judges) knew of Christ's, but while the priests were an impotent minority, the *qadis* administered the laws of the land. The same historian expounds upon the psychological resentment of the clerics:

> To screen themselves from the insults of the populace, the priests did not quit their abodes save in cases of absolute necessity. They often feigned sickness, and lay all day upon their beds, in order to escape payment of the monthly poll-tax enacted by the public treasury. Thus self-condemned to long periods of seclusion, to a solitary and contemplative life, always introspective, they laid up in silence, and with a kind of voluptuous delight, the treasures of their hatred; they felt delight in the daily growth of their rancour and in storing their memories with fresh grievances.

They lived, in fact, in a perpetual state of boredom in which martyrdom glowed.

While the *qadis* were reluctant persecutors, the law they had been trained to enforce punished with death the apostasy of those who had embraced or been born into Islam and those who denied God's existence or insulted His Prophet. Under the reign of Abd-al-Rahman II (822–52), the peril of discussing religion on social occasions was cruelly illustrated. A Cordoban priest named Perfectus, trusting in the license of talk between the literate, allowed himself to discuss with some Muslim acquaintances the respective merits of his faith and theirs. Carried away, the priest dared to impugn the sincerity of Muhammad. This was too much for the consciences of his hearers. Denounced, tried, and sentenced to death, Perfectus was publicly executed on the feast that marked the end of Ramadan, April 18, 850. This heroic spectacle inspired a large number of intransigent souls to self-sacrifice, or self-exhibition. Flora, a virgin of mixed background, was overly influenced by her friendship with Eulogius, a priest, to endorse the religion of her Christian mother and to deny that of her Muslim father. She was followed to the scaffold by Eulogius, as is recounted by his friend Alvaro, a rich layman of Jewish origin but impassioned belief in the Holy Trinity. Alvaro was an angry propagandist. A vivid attack on his Christian contemporaries shows how far most had gone in accepting Arabic culture:

> My fellow-Christians delight in the poems and romances of the Arabs; they study the works of Mohammedan theologians and philosophers, not in order to refute them, but to acquire a correct and elegant Arabic style. Where to-day can a layman be found who reads the Latin Commentaries on Holy Scriptures? Who is there that studies the Gospels, the Prophets, the Apostles? Alas! the young Christians who are most conspicuous for their talents have no knowledge of any literature or language save the Arabic; they read and study with avidity Arabian books; they amass whole libraries of them at a vast cost, and they everywhere sing the praises of Arabian lore. On the other hand, at the mention of Christian books they disdainfully protest that such works are unworthy of their notice. The pity of it! Christians have forgotten their own tongue, and scarce one in a thousand can be found able to compose in fair Latin a letter to a friend! But when it comes to writing Arabic, how many there are who express themselves in that language with the greatest elegance, and even compose verses which surpass in formal correctness those of the Arabs themselves!

Alvaro and his army of martyrs represented the implacable forces that in the long run would reconquer Spain for Catholic Christianity and destroy the triune symbiosis of Muslim, Christian, and Jew. But in the short run the Cordoban martyrs achieved the opposite of what they had surely intended. Outside Spain their relics were sought for the enhancement of churches; inside Spain most ecclesiastics condemned these acts of faith as committing virtual suicide for themselves and placing their fellow Christians in grave danger. Many Mozarabs completed their acceptance of Arab culture by acceptance of the Arabs' religion — not pressed to do so by the authorities, but anxious not to be identified with the troublemakers. Among the Mozarabs who continued to practice Christianity, the exclusive use of Arabic names became increasingly common, even for churchmen. One example of this — and of integration with Islamic culture — was Rabi' ibn-Zaid, Christian bishop of Cordoba around 800.

בעל הבית ונתן בינינו שאומרים יהודה

The Jews adapted themselves even more easily to coexistence with Islam (whose victories they had assisted) than did the Christians. They found much in the religion and culture of the Arabs that appealed to them. The Islamic conception of God — "He begets not nor is He begotten" — was as transcendent as the Judaic. Arabic had affinities not only with Hebrew but with Aramaic, the language that the Jews and the rest of the Middle East had spoken for centuries. But whereas Aramaic had little literature to tempt the Jews, Arabic had a rich and complex poetry and a sophisticated grammar. "The acquisition of the Arab language by the Jew," an Israeli historian, S. D. Goitein, has written, "meant also their adoption of Arab ways of thinking and forms of literature, as well as of Muslim religious notions. Arabic was used by Jews for all kinds of literary activities, not only for scientific and other secular purposes, but for expounding and translating the Bible or the Mishnah [codification of the oral law], for theological and philosophical treatises, for discussing Jewish law and ritual, and even for the study of Hebrew grammar and lexicography." Despite a historical aptitude for philology and linguistics, the Jews in Palestine or Alexandria had never worked out a system of grammar and lexicography for Hebrew. In Andalus, Jewish grammarians Yehuda Hayyuj and Jonah ibn-Janah discovered that all Hebrew words, like Arabic, went back to triliteral roots.

The Jews, it need hardly be emphasized, did not accept the new religion as they did its grammar (though there were some notable converts). They still believed that their own ancient faith was superior, as was argued by Judah ha-Levi, a native of Toledo, in his *Kitab al-Khazari*. In this classic of Judaism, a searching Khazar (from south Russia) discusses the eternal verities with a philosopher, a Christian, and a rabbi respectively. The rabbi wins. But theology apart, the Jews accepted the culture that Islam had produced and prospered within it.

Because of the urban evolution that accompanied Islam, Jews began to excel as physicians, scholars, and artisans. One famous Jew, Hasdai ibn-Shaprut (c. 915– c. 970) worked as treasurer, vizier, and trusted diplomat for the first caliph; he worked as cultural adviser to the second. A co-translator of Dioscorides (a Greek physician of Nero's time), he told Jews in the East such encouraging news of Andalus that many migrated west; a Talmudic school was started in Spain that eclipsed the schools of Iraq (or Babylonia). In secular literature Jews also excelled. Their poetry developed along Arabic lines and their philosophy explored the same themes as those essayed by Muslims.

The readiness of Jews to adopt Arabic names shows the intimacy of the Jewish and Arab cooperation in Andalus. In other countries Jews kept a Hebrew name for synagogal purposes while employing a gentile name in everyday life. In Andalus a different practice began and was maintained in Islamic countries until the twentieth century. The above-quoted S. D. Goitein has written: "Arabic names are used for the same purposes without scruple, and the custom of bearing double names, one in the language of the country and one in Hebrew, is by no means common."

Those in servitude to masters were below, and sometimes above, the Jews and Christians in the social strata. Spain was not only a greedy market for slaves,

One of the typical arts of tenth-century Cordoba was ivory carving, especially of intricate caskets or boxes generally intended to hold jewelry or perfume. The two views of one such box at left show a hunting scene (a sport the Umayyads were devoted to) and (right) a qadi sitting in justice. This example, the top of which is broken, was made about 970 for Cordoba's chief of police.
Overleaf:
The portal on the west side of the Great Mosque of Cordoba was built under the caliph al-Hakam II around 960 and remains an outstanding example of the Islamic genius in the field of ornamentation.

but the place from which slaves (in particular, white slaves and eunuchs) were exported to the rest of the Islamic world. The same Israeli expert has pointed out that the status of slaves among Arabs, as among Jews, differed from their status in the potteries of Athens, the latifundia of Rome, or on the plantations of America. "They were members of the household with more independent status than sons or younger brothers." Certain categories (and in particular the soldier-slaves of the praetorian guard) enjoyed high prestige in Andalus. The Prophet's commendation of those who freed slaves was often earned, and freed slaves had founded families of importance. There were three main sources of slaves: the annual campaigns against the un-Islamized parts of Spain — the slavery would be temporary for those whose families could afford to ransom them; black Africa; and most important, the Black Sea shores, southern Italy, Lombardy, and Galicia. Known as Siklabi (or Slavs), slaves from these regions were imported by Jewish middlemen, often by way of the great slave market in Verdun, and sold in Spanish ports.

One aspect of Islamic slavery, which cannot be justified but which sprang from the dictates of Islamic tradition (though not belief), was the institution of eunuchs. The slaves employed in the royal harem were men who had been gelded in much the same way as tomcats are in modern suburbia. This enabled them to circulate among the women without suspicion. The operation was carried out when the slaves were young, either at Verdun or at the port of Pechina, before they were sent inland. Although the Jewish slave dealers who performed the operation had access to the best

medical knowledge of the day, the mortality rate was high, making the price of a eunuch much greater than that of an ordinary slave. Along with the slaves imported from Africa, the Siklabi eunuchs were given names that belied their condition: Luck, Gaiety, or the names of flowers and precious stones. When slaves were liberated, they became clients of their owners' families; some then became slaveholders themselves. Christians and Jews were allowed to own slaves, provided the slaves were not Muslims.

Although he was not the first Umayyad ruler to surround himself with slaves, Abd-al-Rahman III increasingly entrusted them with the highest positions. Over a comparatively short time the number of slaves at caliphal disposal rose from 3,750 to 13,750. Titles such as "Lord of the Kitchen," "Lord of the Stables," "Lord of the Posts," explain themselves. Apropos of the last, the Umayyad postal service was in advance of its time. While watchtowers on the coast flashed a kind of telegraphy, by the eleventh century pigeons were used for urgent messages. The official correspondence, however, depended on the feet of black slaves, known for their swiftness.

Islamic life at its most typical was urban. It was lived in the civilized town, not the desert, whose nomads never took religion as seriously as the townsmen, nor in the countryside, where agrarian rhythm clashed with the lunar calendar that rules Islam. Baghdad was the great Muslim capital of the ninth century and Cairo of the eleventh, but the tenth century belonged to Cordoba. The greatest geographer of the Middle Ages, al-Idrisi, was himself a descendant of Spanish grandees and a student in Cordoba. His description of the city

is no less valuable for having been written in the century following the greatness of the caliphate, when the city had been "ground in the mill of discord" and its people subjected to great disasters. "Cordoba," he wrote, "is made up of five continuous cities, each surrounded by walls that divide it from the rest, and possessing enough markets, hostelries, baths and buildings for the different professions. From east to west the city covers a distance of three miles. From the Gate of the Jews in the north to the Gate of the Bridge in the south is about one mile." The bridge over the Guadalquivir, which al-Idrisi said surpassed all others for its beauty and solidity of construction, consisted of seventeen arches. His description of the people reveals qualities that were to prove themselves peculiarly and permanently Spanish:

> Among the rest of the Spaniards they are the most advanced in science and the most zealous in piety. . . . They have won fame for the purity of their doctrine, the rigor of their honesty, the formality of their customs in regard to dress, riding accoutrements, elevation of feeling in assemblies and gatherings and finally in often exquisite taste as regards food and drink; add to all this great amiability and perfect manners.

Unlike the Greco-Romans, whose cultural vitality they otherwise revived, the Muslims lacked theaters, academies, and public forums for debate. They spent much time at home. This had one incidental benefit — it encouraged book production. Women as well as men became famous copyists.

The Andalus home survives, not only in contemporary description, but in its direct descendant, the type of house still to be found in certain cities of Morocco, such as Fez. Typical was a characterless exterior, a vast door, and inside a zigzag passage leading to a small patio, paved with stone, or in some cases marble, and shaded by an awning or a vine. One or two rooms opened off this courtyard. Reception rooms, they also served as sleeping quarters for members of the family or household staff. At each end of these rooms there would be a raised niche, screened by a curtain, whose Arabic name *kubba* gives us, by way of the Spanish *alcoba,* the English "alcove."

The furniture was simple and could easily be transported from one room to another. The floors were covered with the same rush mats still used today in Egypt and Iraq; on top of these were spread woolen carpets or animal skins, their hair smoothed short. The walls were hung some six feet high with silk or multicolored wool. Beneath these hangings were long low divans, their mattresses covered with velvet or brocade. Wool cushions were used in winter, to be replaced in the summer by cooler cushions of cloth or leather. The beds were in the alcoves, protected against the dangers of rats or scorpions by being raised above the ground and enclosed by curtains. The beds consisted of a mattress covered with a sheet, a pillow, and a quilt, with a heavier blanket for cold weather.

Instead of wardrobes or cupboards, massive chests, heavily padlocked, were used for storing clothes. The keys to these chests, as well as to the storeroom where such provisions as olive oil, honey, and dried fruits were kept in great corked jars, were carried by the master of the house. Candles or brass lamps lit the houses, charcoal-burning braziers of metal or terra-

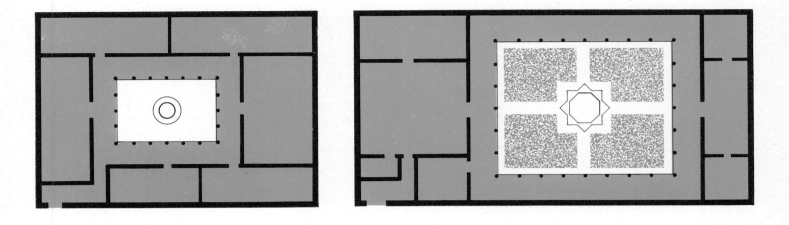

cotta kept them warm. Only the mansions of the rich had private baths; the hot air from the furnaces that heated them was channeled through the living room walls as a form of central heating. But all Muslims — and assimilated Christians and Jews — practiced regular bathing at a time when this was unknown, or frowned on, elsewhere in Europe. A man or woman had to wash before praying, and to wash from head to foot after sexual intercourse. Some nine hundred public baths, or *hammams,* are reported to have served the various quarters of Cordoba. For women, the *hammams* were the equivalent of today's hairdressers, where they would meet their friends, exchange gossip, and show off the fineness of their lingerie. Skilled artists in make-up were available to remove body hair and perfume long, dark tresses with the prized oil of civet. The afternoon was the women's time. During the mornings and evenings adolescent boys scrubbed and soaped the male Cordobans.

The *hammam* represented an unconscious return to the Greco-Roman tradition. Part of that tradition had been the bisexual sensuality found in most Latin poets, not least in the Spanish satirist Martial. In Andalus sexual ambiguity was not confined to one class or sect. The book-loving second caliph (who only produced an heir late in middle age) was famed for his *hubb al-walad* (pederasty); so was a distinguished *qadi;* so was the Jewish poet ibn-Sahl. Those who loved women, and were not married, could have recourse to the *khans* frequented by women of easy virtue, or regular brothels. Nor, despite the Koranic injunctions against alcohol, was Andalus teetotal. From the ninth century on, a wine market leased to a Chris-

tian did brisk business on the outskirts of the capital; its vats supplied a host of cabarets and taverns in which the Andalusian love of music and dancing found exuberant expression.

If Cordoba revived, and in some ways improved, the ease of Roman life, it also revived some of the sterner Roman necessities. Since the "Abode of Peace" (as the Muslims called Islam) was in permanent tension with the adjoining "Abode of War" (Christendom), the needs of defense required a network of roads; excellently built, these usually followed the same routes as their Roman predecessors. Furthermore, after a Norman incursion up the Guadalquivir, a fleet was built by the early Umayyads; under the caliphs, Almeria was a major naval base. The needs of the *hajj,* or pilgrimage — which took place at varying seasons of the year, according to the lunar calendar — also affected communications. Hostels and hospitals for the pilgrims, many of whom traveled all the way on foot, became a necessity.

Spanish Islam thus combined urbanity, in its walled cities, with mobility. This mobility extended to money, the sinews of commercial movement. The first Umayyads struck dirhems of silver, five hundred examples of which have been discovered and identified. Dating from the year in which Abd-al-Rahman III declared himself caliph, the royal mint added to state revenues by striking gold dinars in increasing numbers. The coins never carried a portrait of the ruler. Each side carried a double inscription, one running around the circumference, the other centered. The central inscription on the obverse proclaimed the unity and uniqueness of God; on the reverse, the name and titles

These exterior (below) and interior (right) views of the Great Mosque of Cordoba give scarcely a suggestion of how the building appeared in the tenth century, before a cathedral was erected in its midst and when it formed the vital center of community life. Here the Cordoban came to make his devotions and hear official proclamations. Here, too, were held classes and religious or scholarly debates and discussions. To the caliphs, the Great Mosque was a symbol of the wellsprings of their temporal as well as their religious power.

of the ruler appeared. The circular inscription on the obverse, preceded by the *bismillah,* or invocation, gave the place and date of the coin's striking; the circumference of the reverse carried a verse from the Koran attesting the prophetic mission.

It was appropriate that even the money of Andalus was dominated by religious formulae. Far more durable than Cordoba's houses, *hammams,* and paved, lighted streets, more impressive than the palace-city of Medinat al-Zahra, one building at the center of this capital of twenty-eight suburbs represented the fulcrum of this otherwise urbane and hedonistic society. The Great Mosque of Cordoba — so hugely complete even today that the cathedral erected in its midst by Charles V resembles Jonah engulfed by the whale — bore witness, like the coinage, to Muhammad's mission. The mosque had expanded over the site of a Visigothic church dedicated to Saint Vincent. According to the Arab historian al-Razi, when the Muslims first took Cordoba they followed the practice of Omar I in the East and shared the building with the Christians. But when Cordoba and its Muslim population grew, the structure was no longer large enough for two congregations. Abd-al-Rahman I made an agreement with the Christians whereby they were generously compensated for the original building and authorized to build a new cathedral on the outskirts of the city. A comparatively small mosque was built where the church had stood. Abd-al-Rahman's heir added galleries for women, an ablutions fountain in the external courtyard, and a minaret. This early mosque consisted of nine naves of pillars taken from previously existing buildings. The mosque was again expanded under Abd-al-Rahman II.

The style of the mosque, up till the tenth century, recalled the Middle East, and in particular Syria, where the Umayyads had their roots. But probably inspired by Roman aqueducts (such as the one at Segovia, still intact today) the builders raised the roof — which would have been oppressively low had it rested on the forest of pillars — by superimposing a double row of arcades. The caliph Abd-al-Rahman III, though preoccupied with building his palace-city, nevertheless contributed a minaret of architectural importance, since it formed the model for the later tower-minarets of Seville, Rabat, and Marrakesh, which still survive. (The Cordoban tower, no longer a minaret, was threatened by collapse in 1593; its by then Christian owners preserved it by enclosing it within a campanile, the work being completed in 1618.)

Abd-al-Rahman worked out new stylistic developments which his son, al-Hakam II, was to accomplish during a fifteen-year reign from 961 to 976. These changes reflected the richer, more grandiose style of Abbasid Baghdad. A cupola was erected over the central nave and three others in front of the mihrab. This splendid niche, designed to show the direction of Mecca, was inlaid with mosaics under the direction of experts borrowed from Constantinople. With much stylized carving of floral motifs, with arches intertwined in the vaulting to form series upon series of geometric patterns, a new and richer Andalusian style had been achieved.

This great mosque — the first among the three thousand that Cordoba boasted — became the focus for the city's religious life. It was particularly thronged at the two great feasts of the Islamic year. The first marked

The wealth and power of Caliph Abd-al-Rahman III is symbolized by his gold coinage (left) and by the majestic minaret he added to the Great Mosque, a copy of which (below) still stands in Marrakesh.
Overleaf:
The Muslim prays facing the direction of Mecca, and to orient the congregation properly, a small niche, the mihrab, came to be recessed into the relevant wall of the mosque. Gradually the mihrab came to be considered the holiest part of the mosque and it was embellished accordingly. There is scarcely a mihrab to match that built for al-Hakam II at Cordoba. The glittering gold mosaic dome (left) that surmounts it is a brilliant synthesis of Byzantine and Islamic art, having been constructed by Byzantine craftsmen sent by their emperor at the behest of the caliph. The columns (right) that support the horseshoe arch of the mihrab also show Byzantine influence, especially in the carving of the capitals.

the climax of Ramadan. Ramadan is the holy month observed by day-long fasting, during which the faithful were forbidden to eat, drink, or make love during the daylight hours; it combined austerity with joy in a manner typical of Islam. Every night when the sun sank the city was given over to carnival while the illuminated mosque was thronged with worshipers. Andalus was famous for the abundance and cheapness of its fruits as well as for its pastry and grilled meats. While people made up for what they had lacked by day — before dawn a last hurried meal was consumed to carry them through until the following nightfall — storytellers and colloquial poets, jugglers, and acrobats, performed for the wide-awake. The strenuous month, in which evil emotions were to be avoided as sternly as diurnal appetites, was followed by three days of holiday during which the river was crammed with the pleasure craft of a city released from its normal toil. The second and greater feast, lasting four days, coincided with the pilgrimage to Mecca. This commemorated the great sacrifice that Abraham, the progenitor of the Arabs, had been willing to offer in the life of his son. Every family that could afford to do so celebrated that historic occasion by killing a sheep and dividing its meat among the poor. New clothes were worn and visits exchanged.

The Great Mosque also had an educational function. At a time when even the most exalted in Christendom (unless they were clerics) were illiterate, nearly everyone in Andalus could read and write. A broad system of primary education culminated in the University of Cordoba. Lectures of the university were given in the Great Mosque. As still happens in Cairo's al-Azhar

University, thousands of students thronged the vast, twilit area, forming into groups around teachers in various sections of the mosque.

The intellectual life of Andalus had developed greatly under al-Hakam II. His agents searched Cairo, Baghdad, Damascus, and Alexandria for books to buy or copy for his library. His collection is reputed to have eventually numbered some 400,000 volumes; the catalogue alone occupied forty-four volumes.

One of the students who benefited from this mosque-university was to raise the caliphate to a last peak of political power from which it then fell with unequalled speed. Muhammad ibn-abi-'Amir — his Arabic title al-Mansur, "the Conqueror," caused him to be known to European history as Almanzor — derived from a good family whose fortunes had declined; in his case his roots went back to Yemen. As ambitious as he was brilliant, as guileful as capable, he won his way to power through the favor of the wife of al-Hakam and mother of the caliph's only male heir. When al-Hakam died, his son, Hisham II, was only twelve. Almanzor took possession of the boy and as chamberlain ruled in his name, sequestering him in a new palace, Al-Madina al-Zahira, and spreading the word that the young man (who in reality was sedated with sensual pleasures) had decided to devote himself to religion.

Almanzor established a family despotism that lasted from 978 to 1009. Feared at home for his harshness, he was hated by the Christians in the north for the fifty campaigns he led against them. The contradictions in his character were shown in his most grandiose gesture — the sack of Santiago de Compostela, the spiritual center of Christian resistance. After a campaign in which he was as ruthless to wavering Muslims as to resisting Christians, he and his soldiers entered the shrine of the saint whom the Christians believed had fought in their ranks. The tomb, like the city, was deserted — except for a solitary monk.

"What are you doing here?" Almanzor demanded.

"Praying to Saint James," was the monk's reply.

"Then pray on." While ordering his soldiers to leave the monk in peace and the tomb intact, Almanzor had Christian captives carry the gates of Santiago and the cathedral bells on their backs all of the almost four hundred miles south to Cordoba. (When Cordoba fell to the reconquering Christians, the bells were returned — on the backs of Muslims.)

A builder as much as a soldier, Almanzor was responsible for the last and greatest enlargement of the Great Mosque. During the building he toiled as a common laborer alongside captives and slaves. When he died, he was mourned by many Muslims who remembered his stern justice and his able defense of the realm. But by usurping power he had destroyed the constitutional authority of the Umayyads, whose last seven caliphs, with an average reign of less than eight years, were young or incompetent. For his military campaigns and autocratic power he had relied on a vast army composed of Spanish, Berber, or Negro mercenaries. These praetorians owed allegiance to little but their eyes, which were greedy, and their hands, which were treacherous. As for the Christians, a monkish chronicler expressed their attitude: "Almanzor died in 1002; he was buried in Hell." The sparing of Santiago's tomb was put down, not to good qualities in Almanzor, but to the invincibility of the warrior-saint.

*The medieval Santiago de Compostela — where
the reputed tomb of the apostle Saint James the
Greater was discovered in the ninth century — was
an important sanctuary, ranking only behind
Jerusalem and Rome as a place of pilgrimage.
The apostle himself was considered the patron
saint of the reconquest, thus the conquest and sack
of Santiago de Compostela by Almanzor outraged
Christians, as it was meant to do. Ironically, the
sparing of his shrine was credited to the powers of
the saint rather than the clemency of the conqueror.
The present cathedral was built in the twelfth
century and includes Saint James in his role as the
"Slayer of Moors" (below).*

IV

Intellect and Beyond

The vitality of the culture that evolved in the Spanish caliphal state is attested by its ability to flourish after that state's collapse. Between 1009, when Almanzor's second son and successor was killed, and 1231, when the builder of the Alhambra founded Granada — the last Muslim state on Spanish soil — Andalus experienced three forms of rule, each one of which could have destroyed a less firmly rooted culture. These three were the *taifa* kings, followed by the Almoravides and finally the Almohades.

Although the last Umayyad claimant was not deposed until 1031, the end of caliphal power can be dated twenty-two years earlier, with the extinction of Almanzor's line. Nothing foretold so sudden a collapse. Only a generation earlier the Muslims had inflicted their gravest defeat on their Christian neighbors, the sack of Santiago de Compostela, the very symbol of resistance to Islam. The collapse nevertheless had causes that in retrospect can clearly be discerned. For all their inherited talents, the Umayyads resembled other dynasties in that they made no plans for the continuity of their state once the royal family failed to produce competent rulers. The ineffectiveness of the grandson of Abd-al-Rahman III facilitated the family dictatorship of Almanzor; the ineffectiveness of Almanzor's second son made it easy for his mercenary army of Berbers and slaves to participate in the struggle for power. The latent lawlessness of an overtaxed citizenry was balanced by a lack of responsibility in the aristocracy and upper middle class. Once no strong individual ruled, the unity that the Umayyads had managed to impose on their mixed population crumbled. Warring elements grabbed what they could.

From 1009 until 1091, Andalus was ruled by what became known as the *taifa* kings. A card pack of kinglets — each representing a *taifa,* or faction, each inspired by bigotry for a particular group, or greed for the treasure of the caliphs — ruled an Andalus fragmented into a score of petty states. The rulers represented three basic groups: the Berbers, the Slavs (as white slaves were generically known), and the Andalusians, those Muslims of various origin who had begun to cohere into a homogeneous unity.

The feuding of these small states offered an unhoped-for opportunity to the Christian kingdoms in the north of Spain, previously as divided as the Muslims had become but now united by the prospect of reconquest. A series of Christian victories, capped by the capture in 1085 of Toledo by one of these Christian kings — Alfonso VI of León — frightened the Muslims into turning south. North Africa, until recently a dependency of Andalus, had become the empire of a Sahara-based dynasty (the forebears of the modern Tuaregs) that ruled not only along the Mediterranean from Morocco to western Algeria but south to Mauretania and as far as the basin of the Senegal River. This dynasty acquired its European name, Almoravide, from the Arabic *al-murabitun,* "those who live in religious retreats." (These retreats were, however, the equivalents of military forts.)

The first Almoravides exemplified the Berber devotion to religion. Unfortunately for them, once possessed of Muslim Spain, to which they came as rescuers and in which they stayed as masters, they were quickly softened and corrupted by the temptations of its urbane civilization. After half a century, popular revolts led to

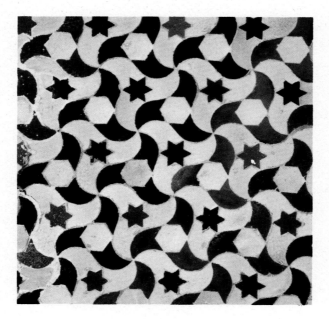

a brief period of renewed anarchy from which Andalus had to be rescued by a second wave of North African saviors. The Almohades — their name also had a religious connotation, meaning "assertors of the unity of God" — were also Berbers, but were from the High Atlas, not the desert. Their founder, ibn-Tumart, was a theologian of some sophistication who had studied in Cordoba as well as Alexandria, Mecca, and Baghdad. After the conquest of Andalus in 1147, five Almohade caliphs ruled, until the death of the last without an heir in 1212 delivered what was left of Muslim Spain to the Christians — except for the small kingdom of Granada, which was a Christian vassal. Although they staved off reconquest for more than a century, neither of these Berber dynasties inspired affection or trust. The Andalusians were used to a different, more urbane approach to religion than the Berbers' simple and passionate faith.

Each of these three periods — that of the *taifa* kings, the Almoravides, and the Almohades — produced men of towering intellect: scientists, in the broad medieval use of the word, whose genius ranged from medicine and geography at one extreme, to philosophy, mysticism, and astrology at the other.

During the time of troubles that marked and followed the collapse of the caliphate, two men, ibn-Hazm (994–1064), a Muslim, and ibn-Gabirol (*c.* 1021–58), a Jew, distinguished themselves in philosophy, which each combined with the writing of poetry. Ibn-Hazm was born in Cordoba of Iberian stock, though he seems to have fabricated for himself a Persian-Arabic ancestry. He was for a time in politics, acting as vizier to Abd-al-Rahman V, one of the last, petty Umayyads. But his

chief importance was as a controversial theologian whose opinions on the Koran led to his compulsory retirement on a country estate. His most important book — a study of various religious sects — gives him a claim to be called the founder of comparative religion.

Ibn-Gabirol was an orphan, of sickly physique, born in Malaga. His poetry was mostly inspired by love and wine, but some is of such exalted character that it has earned a place in the Jewish liturgy. Ibn-Gabirol differed from most other Jewish thinkers of his day (and in a sense foreshadowed Spinoza) in treating general philosophic subjects. His approach was inspired by the last great intellectual movement of the classical world, Neoplatonism, for which he is known as the Jewish Plato. His philosophical dialogue, translated from Arabic into Latin as *Fons Vitae,* "The Fountain of Life," was to exert a greater influence on Christians, in particular on Duns Scotus and the Franciscans, than on his co-religionists. A thousand years earlier, another Jewish scholar, Philo of Alexandria, had orientalized Platonic philosophy, thus making possible its absorption into the thought of Christianity and Islam. Now in the eleventh century ibn-Gabirol — known in Christendom as Avicebrón — reoccidentalized the Greco-Muslim philosophy current in Spain and restored it to Europe.

The Almoravides — bigoted to start with and corrupt at the finish — could not produce a climate of intellectual confidence. A new tang of intolerance was in the Spanish air on both sides of the confessional divide. In the Christian north, the Cluniac monks favored by Constance, the wife of Alfonso VI, stood for an intransigently Christian view as against the tolerance of

the king. In the Muslim south, the North African and Negro warriors distrusted Christians; after the Muslim reconquest of Valencia, for example, they made the atmosphere so uncongenial that the local Mozarabs migrated north.

Against this background of fanaticism and then corruption, ibn-Bajjah (or Avempace) gave the significant title of *The Hermit's Regime* to his most important work. Expressive of the perennial disgust of the man of integrity with established corruption, the book, with its philosophy of aloof withdrawal, was to have an increasing influence on the better spirits of Andalus. Yet ibn-Bajjah was no otherworldly recluse. A leading figure in the revolt against the Ptolemaic system of astronomy, he also kept up a learned correspondence on medicine with a Muslim member of the Judaeo-Spanish ibn-Hasdai family who lived in Cairo.

If ibn-Bajjah commended a flight inward, two other thinkers took refuge from Almoravide tyranny in describing the world outside. In his *Description of North Africa*, al-Bakri — a member of an Arab family that had worked for the Umayyads — wrote the first detailed account of the Sudan, the "land of the blacks" to the south of the Sahara. A still greater geographer, al-Idrisi, was descended from an Arab family that had fallen from power in Malaga as a result of the Almoravide invasion. Born in Ceuta, across the straits in Morocco, al-Idrisi was educated at the University of Cordoba but thereafter traveled widely in Africa and the Middle East. He was to die in Norman-ruled Palermo in 1166 — exactly a century after other Normans had invaded England. His most famous work was dedicated to King Roger II, who ruled a Muslim and Christian society

in Sicily. Entitled in Arabic, "The delight of him who desires to journey through the climates," but generally referred to as *Roger's Book,* it gave the most elaborate description of the world available to medieval man. Previous Islamic geographies were largely prompted by pilgrimage and concentrated on the Muslim countries. *Roger's Book* contained much accurate information about European countries.

Many of the versatile geniuses who dominated the Middle Ages today inspire little more than respect for their accomplishments. Although they contributed to an evolving science, evolution has inexorably dated much of their information and the method of most of them. However, ibn-Bajjah's defense of an inner religion in *The Hermit's Regime* inspired one writer whose words can still be read with interest. Ibn-Tufail was born in Guadix, near Granada, in about 1100. Like so many medieval Muslim thinkers, he worked in various fields; he served as a physician at the court of the second Almohade caliph, Abu-Ya'qub Yusuf I (1163–84), and like ibn-Bajjah, he was an astronomer.

But one short allegorical tale — *Hayy ibn-Yaqzan,* or "The Living One, Son of the Vigilant" — made him a forerunner of the Age of Reason. It is probable that the book's translation into European languages — Simon Ockley published an English version under the title *The Improvement of Human Reason* in 1708 — influenced such creators of the modern world as Rousseau and Voltaire. In one aspect the book foreshadowed Kipling's *The Jungle Book,* since ibn-Tufail's hero, like Mowgli, is raised by an animal, though in his case it is a gazelle on a desert island and not a wolf in the jungle. The basic problem posed by

The stylized lions and camels on the coronation
robe (left) of the Norman king of Sicily, Roger II,
show the extent of Arab influence on that monarch.
One of the towering figures at Roger's court was
al-Idrisi, one of the greatest medieval geographers,
whose map of the world (below) looks upside
down to modern eyes, with north at the bottom.
The body of water at right is the Mediterranean,
with the Arabian peninsula above it protruding
upwards into the Indian Ocean. Al-Idrisi also wrote
on botany and materia medica and left copious
descriptions of plants and animals.

In the courtyards and galleries of the mosques of Islam, students gathered around teachers to form a kind of university. In one such gallery (right) at Cordoba, the philosopher ibn-Rushd (known in the West as Averroës) was attacked by a mob inflamed by stricter theologians and banished from Cordoba for his unorthodox views. A delightfully muddleheaded Christian sketch (left) shows ibn-Rushd in a deep discussion of dietary abstinence with the third-century Greek philosopher Porphyry (ibn-Rushd died in 1198).

the book is whether a child, raised without contact with other human beings, can arrive at truth through the unaided use of uncorrupted reason. Ibn-Tufail's conclusion is that he can and that the existence and goodness of God can be inferred without the intervention of revelation — though after his hero visits an inhabited island he concludes that holy books can restrain a humanity whose appetites are its de facto god.

It is at first sight surprising to find such speculative ideas achieving publication under a North African caliph (a contemporary of England's Henry II) who outwardly enforced a rigorous version of orthodox Islam. But just as a Christmas atmosphere blended with the daytime austerities of Ramadan, so speculation flourished at the court of a ruler who upheld religion for the sake of public well-being. An Arab historian describes the Almohade caliph's ceaseless search for books from all parts of Andalus and North Africa and his relaxed manner of discussing even the thorniest of philosophical problems.

Ibn-Tufail introduced the caliph to one of the outstanding intellects of all time, ibn-Rushd (or Averroës), who has left his own account of this first meeting. The caliph asked him his opinion on whether the heavens were eternal or created in time.

> The Commander of the Faithful noticed my embarrassment and turning to Ibn Tufail began discussing with him the question he had put to me. He recalled what Aristotle, Plato and all the philosophers had said on the point, and stated also the arguments brought against them . . . , displaying such copious knowledge as I should not have expected from an expert.

Ibn-Rushd's fame is based on his commentaries on Aristotle, which led indirectly to the scholastic revival in Western Europe. Typical of his philosophical approach was his solution to the conundrum put to him by the caliph. In it he tried to reconcile the Aristotelian doctrine of the eternity of the world (which seemed to deny Creation) with the creationism implicit in Muslim (or for that matter Christian and Jewish) theology. God, he says, is eternal and his creative effort is perpetual. He creates time (or duration) as well as the world, and He may have created it from all eternity, inasmuch as He is Himself without cause. The sophistication of this doctrine can be seen by the ease with which it can be adapted to include the notion of evolution.

The background and career of this greatest philosopher of medieval Spain were typical of his age. His grandfather had been a distinguished theologian as well as *qadi* and *imam* of the Great Mosque of Cordoba; his father, too, had been a *qadi*. Ibn-Rushd studied law and medicine at Cordoba. After a year in Marrakesh (the city that gave its name to Morocco), he served as *qadi* of Seville, then of Cordoba, while in his early forties. Ten years later he was named court physician to succeed ibn-Tufail. The disapprobation that he had feared in his first interview with the caliph was incurred under his successor and ibn-Rushd was banished from Morocco to a town near Cordoba; his works, except for the strictly scientific, were ordered burned. After a reconciliation, he was recalled to Marrakesh where he died, in 1198, at the age of seventy-two.

As a physician, though less important than ibn-Sina, ibn-Rushd composed a medical encyclopedia whose seven books dealt with anatomy, physiology, general

pathology, diagnosis, materia medica, and general therapeutics. He wrote a commentary on Galen's account of fevers and recognized that no one is taken ill twice with smallpox; in ophthalmology, he understood the function of the retina. Like ibn-Bajjah and ibn-Tufail, he also wrote on astronomy. But all these activities were dwarfed by his philosophical works. Ever since the dawn of Islamic philosophy in the ninth century, the central problem had been how to reconcile religion with Aristotle, who enjoyed quasi-prophetic authority. The problem had been compounded by the proliferation of spurious works attributed to Aristotle. Ibn-Rushd got nearer to Aristotle's true thought than had any of his predecessors or contemporaries.

Ibn-Rushd came at the end of the vigorous period of Islamic thought; his greatest influence was on Jewish philosophy, then on Christian. His contemporary and fellow Cordoban, the Jewish philosopher Maimonides (also known as Moses ben Maimon, or ibn-Maimun in Arabic) followed much the same path in the same direction. Both these philosophic giants strove to reconcile their religions with Aristotelian philosophy and, despite doctrinal differences, their problems were essentially the same. Like ibn-Rushd, Maimonides wrote in Arabic, though his works were quickly translated into Hebrew. His *Guide of the Perplexed* (written in Arabic between 1187 and 1190 and translated into Hebrew in southern France some fourteen years later) was, according to the historian George Sarton, "designed to reconcile Jewish theology with Muslim Aristotelianism, or faith with reason."

As precursors of the modern scientific spirit, ibn-Rushd and Maimonides dominated one extreme in the rich cultural harmony of Andalus. The other extreme — that of the mystics, or Sufis — was preoccupied with the search for different, more interior forms of knowledge. Its dominant figure was ibn-Arabi, the greatest mystical visionary of Islamic Spain.

Ibn-Rushd met ibn-Arabi when the latter was still an adolescent. To the younger man we owe an account of this unusual encounter between contrasted geniuses; its enigmatic style is typical of Sufi writing.

I spent a good day in Cordoba at the house of Abu al-Walid Ibn Rushd. He had expressed a desire to meet me in person, since he had heard of certain revelations I had received. . . . I was at the time a beardless youth. As I entered the house the philosopher rose to greet me with all the signs of friendliness and affection, and embraced me. Then he said to me "Yes!" and showed pleasure, on seeing that I understood him. I, on the other hand, being aware of the motive for his pleasure, replied, "No!" Upon this, Ibn Rushd drew back from me, his colour changed and he seemed to doubt what he had thought of me. He then put to me the following question, "What solution have you found as a result of mystical illumination and divine inspiration? Does it coincide with what is arrived at by speculative thought?" I replied, "Yes and no. Between the Yea and the Nay the spirits take their flight beyond matter, and the necks detach themselves from their bodies." At this Ibn Rushd became pale and I saw him tremble as he muttered the formula, "There is no power save from God." This was because he had understood my allusion.

This forward young man had been born in Murcia,

Ibn-Rushd, flanked by two disciples, appears in a detail (below) from The Triumph of Saint Thomas Aquinas, *presumably commemorating the intellectual debt the Angelic Doctor owed to the Islamic sage. Ibn-Rushd considered Aristotle's work as God's supreme revelation of secular truth and in complete accord with religion. His voluminous commentaries on the Greek philosopher are genuinely original works, and embody a heroic attempt to reconcile the positivism of Aristotle with the teachings of Islam.*

in eastern Spain, in 1165. His family was distinguished and, as its name suggests, of Arab origin. His father was probably vizier to a local ruler of Christian descent who managed to resist the invading Almohades until ibn-Arabi was eight. The child was then removed to Seville where Abu-Ya'qub Yusuf (the caliph who had discussed philosophy with ibn-Tufail and ibn-Rushd) took him under his protection. After the typical literary education of those days — in the Koran and its exegesis, the Sayings of the Prophet, religious law, and Arabic grammar and composition — he worked for a time as secretary to the governor. He then fell in love with his first wife, Miryam, and married her. So far there was nothing particularly remarkable in his career. But he and Miryam were linked by a common attraction to the Folk of God, as the Sufis were known. Ibn-Arabi himself tells us that he was initiated into their way when he was twenty.

Like most of the great movements that influence mankind, Sufism must be considered on two levels — as a system of ideas and as a response to social or historic forces. As a system of ideas, the Way of the Sufis — intended to lead the soul to a direct experience of God — had a double source. The life of Muhammad with his practice of nightlong prayer, such verses in the Koran as "Wherever ye turn, there is the face of God," and reputed Sayings — these were evidence to Sufis that the Prophet was at least in part a mystic and that his view of the world was close to theirs. The trouble with the Sayings was that many had been fabricated as support for particular points of view. One respected Saying does give as good an explanation for why God created the world as has been advanced by anyone: "I

was a hidden treasure, and I desired to be known, so I created the creatures that I might be known."

Sufism also had roots outside Islam, in the practice of Christian hermits (of whom Muhammad himself had been aware) and in the writings of a sixth-century Neoplatonic philosopher, Dionysius the Areopagite. Dionysius had been erroneously identified by Christians with one of Saint Paul's Athenian converts in Acts and therefore, in an age that valued authority, he acquired semiapostolic status. He taught the unknowableness of God and the hierarchical nature of the universe, rising by degrees from matter through man, and then the angels, to God. Translated from Greek through Syriac into Arabic, his texts taught the first wave of Islamic mystics to practice penance and mortification. They became known as Sufis — from *suf*, the ordinary word for wool, because they wore plain garments, not robes of silk.

Socially, Sufism was inspired by discontent with the actual world, or the way in which its affairs were misconducted. It had flourished first in Abbasid Iraq, as a movement against an autocratic government. In Spain, the breakdown of the caliphate and the various tyrannies that followed inspired similar protests. One of ibn-Arabi's uncles had been a ruler until his encounter with a Sufi. "Is it right for me to pray in these fine clothes I am wearing?" the ruler asked the Sufi. The latter laughed in derision. In his eyes, he said, the ruler was like a dog sniffing around in the blood of a dead animal and eating it with all its corruption, but lifting its leg when it urinates, lest it soil its body. "You are full of unlawfulness and you ask me about your clothes, when the sufferings of men are upon your head."

The map opposite shows Spain and North Africa
under the Muslims. By the ninth century the lines
between Christian and Muslim were fairly set. The
Christian domains were north of a line running
roughly along the banks of the Douro to the
heights of Osma, then curling northeastward into
Gascony. The Muslim lands were south of a
frontier that ran from Coimbra to Toledo and
Guadalajara, then northward to Pamplona. In
between was a depopulated no-man's-land known
as the Marches, guarded by border fortresses.

This story — and ibn-Arabi reports several others of similar import — shows that Sufism represented a much-needed radical element in Islam.

The widespread diffusion of Sufism in Andalus is attested to by a book that ibn-Arabi wrote much later in his long life, after he had left Spain forever. Remembering the Sufis he had known as a young man, he composed *The Spirit of Holiness in the Counseling of the Soul,* vivid pen portraits of some seventy mystics, male and female, he had known in Andalus. Some of the portraits emphasize the homely wonders that the Sufis could work. Other portraits stress the constancy in prayer, humility, or spiritual love of those portrayed.

Ibn-Arabi left Andalus in middle age to make the pilgrimage to Mecca. He never returned. Instead he divided the rest of his life among such Muslim cities as Fez, Cairo, Jerusalem, Hebron, Mecca, Medina, Baghdad, Konya, and Damascus, where he died at the age of seventy-five. While in Mecca he fell in love with Nizam, the daughter of a local dignitary. She inspired him to write his most famous book of poems, *The Interpreter of Longings.* This work marks a decisive shift in the history of Sufism. While ibn-Tufail had already concluded that man could reach God through the contemplation of nature, ibn-Arabi went further and taught that the existence of creatures exemplifies the essence of the Creator's existence. All things emanate from a divine foreknowledge in which they existed from eternity. In the poems inspired by Nizam — in what was a pure love, he assured his critics — he carried to the ultimate point a rapturous blurring of creation with its creator, where everything stands for something else, where the lover becomes the beloved:

> She said: it astounds me, a self-approving
> lover who walks with pride among flowers
> in a garden.
> I answered: what you've seen should not
> astound you: you have seen yourself in
> the mirror of a person.

An authority on Sufism explains that "flowers" mean created things, and "a garden" means the unitive station, or the poet's essence. The force that unites is love and one of its qualities is that it is unconfined:

> My heart can assume any form:
> a monastery for monks, a pasture
> for gazelles:
> A shrine for idols, the pilgrims' Kaaba:
> the Torah's tablets, the book of
> the Koran.
> My religion's the religion of love —
> where its camels turn,
> there is my faith, there is my religion.

A resurgent Europe was to be inspired by ibn-Rushd and Maimonides; the blend of faith with reason was to power a civilization relying more and more on science in the sense of technology. The East moved in a reverse direction. The crushing military defeats of Islam — the fall of Cordoba in 1236, four years before ibn-Arabi's death, the sack of Baghdad by the Mongols twenty-two years later — inclined more and more Muslims to follow the teachings of ibn-Arabi. Through his life and work Andalus made a decisive contribution to the East. The Andalusian visionary not only linked the earlier form of Sufism with the later, but was himself the bridge between the Sufism of Andalus and that of the East, especially Persia and Turkey.

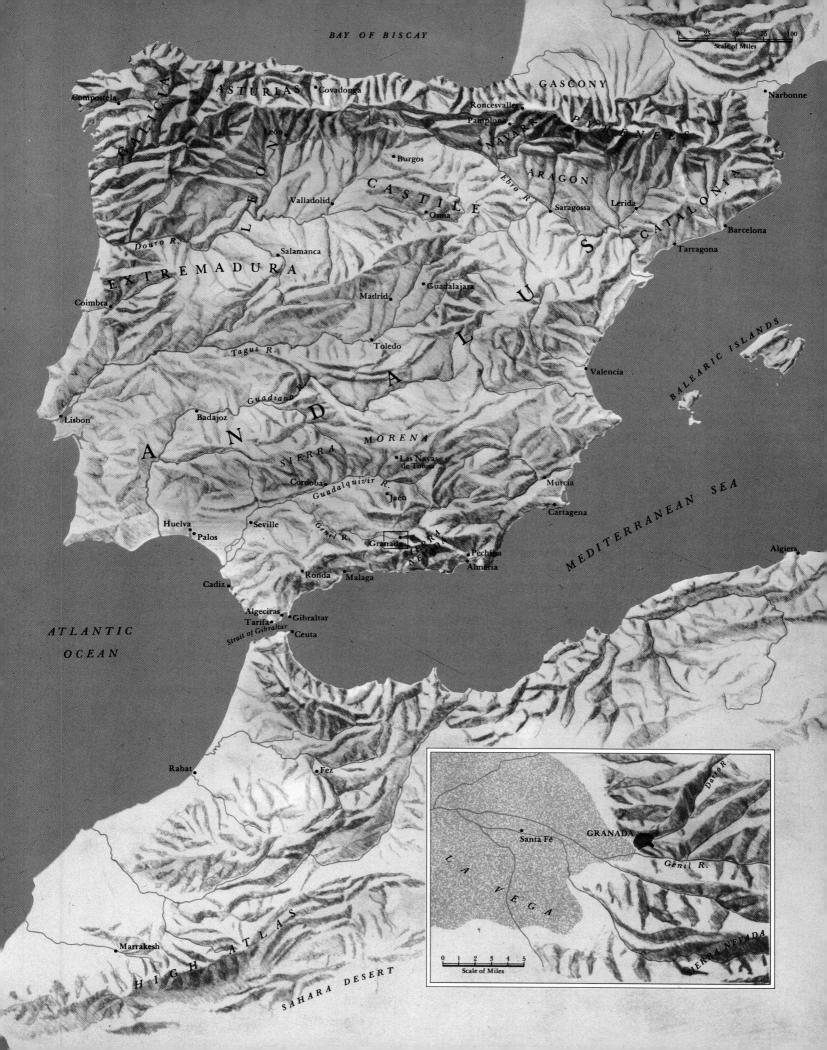

BAY OF BISCAY

ATLANTIC
OCEAN

MEDITERRANEAN SEA

Scale of Miles
0 25 50 75 100

GALICIA

ASTURIAS
Covadonga

GASCONY

Narbonne

Compostela

León

Roncesvalles
Pamplona

PYRENEES

Burgos

NAVARRE

ARAGON

CATALONIA

Ebro R.

Saragossa

Lerida

Valladolid

Osma

CASTILE

Tarragona

Barcelona

Douro R.

Salamanca

EXTREMADURA

Coimbra

Madrid

Guadalajara

A

Toledo

Valencia

BALEARIC ISLANDS

Tagus R.

Lisbon

Badajoz

N

Guadiana R.

D

MORENA

SIERRA

A

Las Navas
de Tolosa

Murcia

Cordoba

Guadalquivir R.

Jaén

Cartagena

Huelva

Seville

Palos

Genil R.

L

SIERRA

Granada

NEVADA

Pechina

Almeria

Algiers

Cadiz

Ronda

Malaga

Algeciras
Tarifa

Gibraltar

Strait of Gibraltar

Ceuta

Rabat

Fez

HIGH ATLAS

Marrakesh

SAHARA DESERT

Santa Fé

LA VEGA

GRANADA

Genil R.

Darro R.

SIERRA NEVADA

Scale of Miles
0 1 2 3 4 5

V

The Spanish Bridge

If Europe's early Middle Ages were dark, exclusion from two sources of light made them so. Exclusion from the first, Europe's Greco-Roman heritage, was in part Europe's own doing; a near-barbarian yet Christian present severed itself from this heritage through theological prejudice. The Church had emerged from a long and bitter struggle as the one institution to survive the upheavals that destroyed the Roman Empire. Because the Church had been persecuted, many of its leaders felt hostility for the pagan culture that had sustained its persecutors, a hostility that was as intense in the parts of the Christian world that read its Scriptures in Greek — the Byzantine empire — as in the parts that read them in Latin. Except for Plato, who had early been absorbed into Christian theology, and Vergil, whose fourth eclogue seemed to prophesy Christ, the pagan authors were neglected and increasingly lost. Some survived through the lucky accident of a parchment being whitened over for the transcription of a saint's life or a sermon; many of the greatest, such as the poetess Sappho, survive in the few verses quoted in a work of criticism. The age when Aegean thinkers had posed many of the major questions and given convincing answers to a number of them was as forgotten as a statue thrown into a cesspool.

Exclusion from the second source of light was caused by a geographical separation — from the sunnier shores of the Mediterranean, and this was due to Europe's physical weakness after the invasions by Goths, Vandals, and Huns. The coming of Islam in the seventh century transformed the Mediterranean from a link to a barrier. In Roman times, even in the chaotic years toward the end, Egyptian monks could journey to northern Ireland while Gauls could visit Syria or Cyrenaica. But after the coming of Islam, Europe was isolated in a winter of rushlights and its intellectual nutriment was of the sparest.

European resurgence was to come only when the two gulfs — between the classical past and the East — were again traversable. In this process bridges of different kinds were to serve. Southern Italy's proximity to Africa made it one such bridge; the Crusades, which propelled young Westerners into creative interaction with the Middle East, was another. More important than either was Andalus.

That this should have been so is one of the ironies of history. To the Europeans who witnessed the astonishing advance of the Arabs and Berbers to the Pyrenees and beyond, who acclaimed the victory of Charles Martel as a last-ditch triumph against Satan, it would have seemed that only evil could result from the loss of Spain. But with the reality of the loss of Spain, the consolidation of a Muslim state in southwest Europe was to create a display case for the best in Middle Eastern culture. The tolerance of Umayyad Andalus was an initially decisive factor. The Mozarabs, those Christians who had adopted Arab culture and who were permitted to live in large communities under their own institutions, were thus enabled to play a pioneer role in the diffusion of Islamic culture to Western Europe, either when they traveled or later, when they found themselves once more under Christian rule. Thanks to them, to the Jews, who were also allowed to live their own lives unmolested, and to the centuries during which Europe accepted the existence of an Arab state flourishing on its territory, the West became

aware that far from being barbarians, the subjects of the caliph enjoyed an enviably higher standard of culture than they knew themselves. Of course, this did not convert them to Islam; but it prepared them to accept treatment by its physicians, to be influenced by its art, and to import what they could of its military methods, its foods, and its pastimes. Far off in a Saxon convent the nun Roswitha of Gandersheim was to pay a telling compliment when she referred to Cordoba as "the ornament of the world."

More ornamentation than the fountains in the caliph's palace came to Andalus from the Middle East. In literature, particularly poetry, the Muslims of Spain regarded the writers of Iraq as their models, and in other fields they readily admitted their debts to non-Arabs. Although centered on a god who had revealed himself in Arabic, Islam fostered a humanism of its own. All mankind was seen as the creation of the One God, who had sent different messengers to different peoples. Culture was regarded as much a product of those who had lived in Ignorance (the technical term used by Islam for pre-Islamic Arabia, and by implication for Greco-Roman paganism) and of such believers in Scripture as Jews and Christians as of the Muslims. Andalus was enabled to become a major bridge between West and East precisely because it saw itself as part of a vaster whole; although a separate state, it was not exclusive in the manner of modern nations.

In purveying the lost Greco-Roman sciences to Western Europe, Spain was acting as a bridge for cargo that originated farther east. The scientific texts that were to reilluminate Europe had been saved from oblivion in Iraq, due to the happy chance that one

Christian sect, the Nestorians, lived on the fringes of the Byzantine empire and had rescued the ancient writings disregarded by their Byzantine oppressors. When Iraq became the central province of the Abbasid empire in the mid-eighth century, its rulers, for practical reasons at first, such as concern for their own health — Greek medicine being a major subject in question — initiated a rarely paralleled impetus for translation. Under the patronage of Baghdad, an astonishing number of classical manuscripts passed by way of the Syriac spoken by the Nestorians into Arabic. Because Arabic was the lingua franca of a vast area, and because there was great mobility inside this area, these texts became the common property of the many scholars who were at that time living in Spain.

More was involved than the simple rescue of ancient authors. Muslims also made significant contributions to the ancient works. Although Galen enjoyed almost religious authority in medicine, one Iraqi physician took advantage of a famine in Egypt to investigate a corpse (dissection was normally forbidden by religious law) and put Galen right on the structure of the human jawbone. Greater original advances were made in the mathematical sciences for which both Arabs and Persians had a special aptitude. An entirely new subject, algebra, was added to the classical arithmetic and geometry, its name deriving from the Arabic title — *'ilm al-jabr wa'l-muqabala* — of a book by al-Khwarizmi, its pioneer. Algebra would hardly have been possible with the letter numbers used by the Romans. Al-Khwarizmi's name was corrupted into algorism, which came to describe a mathematical procedure based on a new system of numerals that reached Europe

The use of the system of numerals called — in the West — Arabic and the adoption of the Indian concept of zero enabled the Muslims to make sophisticated calculations impossible for those Europeans using cumbersome Roman numerals. Complicated geographical and astronomical computations measuring the extent of the earth and the passage of the planets were codified in the eleventh century in the Toledan Tables — a compilation made in Toledo by astronomers including al-Zarqali. A late thirteenth-century French recension of the tables (below, left) was to prove useful to astronomers and navigators alike. Al-Zarqali also improved the astrolabe (right), a navigational instrument that in Christian hands made possible the voyages of exploration of the fifteenth and sixteenth centuries.

Tabula inuencionis tempus arabum

in a complete form via Italy in the twelfth century. An earlier system was used in Spain at least two centuries before. Known as *ghobar* — from an Arabic word for dust — it seems to have been associated with a table of spread sand used for calculation. Initially it did not include the zero.

Four great individuals may symbolize the utility of the Spanish bridge from the tenth century until the thirteenth, when Europe was already poised for its great age of physical and intellectual advance: a mathematician who was also the first French pope; a scholar-translator as prolific as a modern writer of detective fiction; a Spanish king with an enviable title; and the greatest European poet between Vergil and Shakespeare. All four owed much to Andalus.

The life of the first, christened Gerbert, spanned the glory of the caliphate. Born around 940 in the Auvergne, Gerbert received a literary education at the Benedictine monastery of Saint Gerauld in Aurillac. When he had absorbed all that the limited Latin texts available there had to offer, Gerbert had the good fortune to be chosen by his abbot to accompany the visiting count of Barcelona back to the Spanish Marches. In northeast Spain he was within the Andalusian field of influence. If he did not study at Cordoba itself (though one chronicler asserts that he did) the bishopric of Vich to which he was attached was no great distance from Saragossa, then an important Muslim city. He certainly read Arabic books in translation and is later described as using an abacus with ciphers, instead of counters, which suggests his familiarity with the *ghobar* numerals. In 970, Gerbert traveled to Rome with his bishop and so impressed the pope with his knowledge of music

Stargazers have long craned their necks to locate and identify such constellations as the Big and Little Dipper and Orion in the clear night sky, the names and configurations mostly coming down to us from the ancient Greeks. Medieval Islam had its own configurations, again largely based on those of the Greeks. In the late tenth century in Baghdad, Abd-al-Rahman al-Sufi published a treatise on the fixed stars that soon became as indispensable to watchers in the night in Andalus as in Iraq. Three illustrations from a thirteenth-century Moroccan edition of that work are shown on these pages.

Alfonso VI showed his true temper in not only calling himself Emperor of the Two Religions (by which he meant Christianity and Islam) but, in his last years, in cohabiting with a Muslim princess. He was equally tolerant to Jews. His private physician was a Jew and enjoyed great influence at court. His armies, one authority tells us, contained large numbers of Jews and on one occasion military operations were postponed until after the conclusion of the Sabbath. In the mixed society over which he presided, Christians dressed like Arabs and used the *hammams* that had been built under Islam, and nascent Castilian (the future Spanish) filled itself with Arabic words and phrases. Thus the tradition of toleration into which El Sabio was born was fairly well established.

On his mother's side — she was a Hohenstaufen — El Sabio was heir to a yet more startling tradition. Two years before his reign began, his mother's cousin, the emperor Frederick II, had been buried in the cathedral of Palermo, another city on the frontier between Christendom and Islam. The tunic in which he was interred bore an Arabic inscription embroidered in gold. More than any other ruler in history Frederick had created a personal synthesis between East and West. His mixed court was more Muslim in style than Christian — his intellectual collaborators, his courtiers, his dancing girls, his harem, the black slaves who sounded the trumpets in his cortege, were outward signs of Arab influence on him. Frederick's works for science and the arts were outstanding. In 1224 he had founded the University of Naples, its intellectual fuel a rich collection of Arabic manuscripts. Under his patronage ibn-Rushd's commentaries on Aristotle were translated

A prime example of a Christian monarch emulating his Muslim neighbors is Alfonso X, king of León and Castile, who aspired to rule a state as enlightened as those of his colleagues to the south. In his attempt to disseminate knowledge, he had many Arabic works translated not into the Latin of scholars, but into the Romance tongue his people spoke every day. The amenities of his court (left) were not to be matched in Western Europe until much later. He also translated a book on chess and related board games, from which the picture below is taken. Published in 1283, it introduced chess to the West. The seriousness with which the game was played may be inferred from the removal by the players of their shoes, but not their weapons.

such as Adelard of Bath and Robert of Ketton, and Germans such as Hermann the Dalmatian worked in collaboration with Spanish translators, both Christians and Jews. By 1175 Gerard had rendered the Almagest into Latin, and it then became widely known in Europe. But this was only one among a host of translations to which he put his name. Among the subjects he tackled were logic, philosophy, Greek mathematics and astronomy, Arabic mathematics, physics and mechanics, Greek medicine, Arabic medicine, Arabic astrology, alchemy, and geomancy. Among the authors he translated from Arabic into Latin were the philosophers al-Kindi and al-Farabi, and the mathematicians Euclid, Archimedes, and al-Khwarizmi.

The list of Gerard's translations is so enormous — a biography by his pupils claimed seventy-one, but a modern historian of science has listed eighty-seven — that it poses the question of whether all could have possibly been done by him. The probable answer is that he ran a translation workshop, assisted by Jewish and Christian colleagues, as well as by paid apprentices and subordinates. Like the medieval and Renaissance painters who employed apprentices to rough in the body of a religious painting but reserved particularly difficult features for their own touch, he may only have polished much that passed for his work. That Gerard's personal touch took him out of the category of ordinary translators is shown — to take only one example — by his version of Euclid. The Alexandrian geometrician had already been translated by Adelard of Bath, the English traveler and explorer of science of the previous century. But whereas Adelard kept the Arabic terms for geometrical figures, Gerard (through using a ninth-

century translation by ibn-Qurra) introduced such Greek terms as "rhombus" to the West. He thus anticipated a growing tendency for European scholars to be more precise in their borrowings from Greece, and finally to translate only from Greek itself. Gerard was influential in many fields. His translation of *The Canon,* an immense medical encyclopedia by ibn-Sina which was to remain a European textbook until the seventeenth century, introduced a new series of medical terms to the West, ranging from "retina" and "clavicula" to "true" and "false" ribs.

Gerard is only the most outstanding of a host of other translators. Marc of Toledo, for example, was a Spanish physician and priest who translated the Koran and also a book on the pulse. That these translations made Toledo a quintessential symbol of the Spanish bridge was in large part due to the kings who made it their capital. One of these, Alfonso X, who ruled Castile and León from 1252 to 1284, has won a rare accolade from history in his surname El Sabio, "the Wise." He did not win this sobriquet through being successful or adroit — he was neither a military conqueror nor a particularly skilled politician. He won it for his intelligent patronage of learning, and in particular of the transfer of Islamic ideas to Europe.

El Sabio (as it will be convenient to call him to distinguish him from the many other Alfonsos in Spanish history) had much in his family tradition to inspire him to patronize Muslim learning. Alfonso VI (who had captured Toledo in 1085) had continued to use Arabic as an official language and had minted coins modeled on those of Andalus. Although his second wife, Constance of Burgundy, had patronized the Cluniacs,

The healing arts came in for considerable respect in medieval Islam, in contrast to the West where they had fallen into desuetude. The works of such Greek physicians as Galen and Hippocrates were translated into Arabic, and ibn-Sina (known in the West as Avicenna) was only one of many influential Arab doctors and medical writers. If the surgical instruments that were used (below, right) look somewhat alarming, they nonetheless represented the best of their time, as even Christians openly acknowledged. In Sicily, King William II was attended not only by a Muslim physician, but by a Muslim astrologer, both of whom were present at his death (below, left).

and astronomy that he was launched on what became a great teaching career.

Made head of the cathedral school at Reims, Gerbert revived the liberal arts curriculum, the *trivium* and *quadrivium*, which had fallen into desuetude but was to become the basic curriculum of the Middle Ages. Although both disciplines went back to Saint Augustine in the fifth century and the Visigothic Saint Isidore of Seville in the seventh, it was not these Christian forebears but the inspiration of Cordoba, where the tradition had been continued, that encouraged Gerbert to reintroduce them into Europe. The *trivium* comprised grammar, rhetoric, and logic; the *quadrivium* combined arithmetic, geometry, astronomy, and music. After becoming archbishop of Reims in 991, then of Ravenna in 998, Gerbert was elected pope as Sylvester II in 999. He was, with his more limited means, as zealous a collector of books and manuscripts as the caliph al-Hakam. Not surprisingly, his scientific interests — he constructed planetary globes, organs, and sundials — and his indifference to the early fathers won him the reputation of a black magician.

A century was to pass before the impetus given to science by Gerbert was accelerated, again from Spain. In 1114, a boy, Gerard, was born in the Italian city of Cremona; he was destined to become the greatest translator of all time. As a young man Gerard left Italy for Spain through the desire to read the Almagest, the Arabic version of Ptolemy's great treatise on astronomy, which was not yet available in Latin. He studied Arabic in Toledo, which had been reconquered for Christendom in 1085 and turned by a great archbishop, Raimondo, into a major center of translation. Englishmen

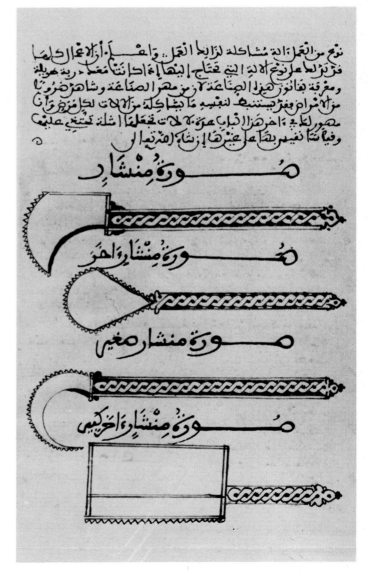

into Latin, and Muslim and Jewish philosophers, mathematicians, and astronomers thronged his court. Abuzz with Arab poets, Palermo became, according to Dante, the birthplace of Italian vernacular poetry.

Thus El Sabio, Alfonso X, grew up in a society that accepted plurality and in a family tradition that was intoxicated with Semitic culture. On ascending the throne he personally assumed direction of the work of translation. Since he was himself multilingual, El Sabio took part, as an equal, in the discussions of the learned, whatever their faith. While continuing to encourage the scientific work of his predecessors, he also encouraged the translation of popular works. In this he was extending the work of his father, Ferdinand III, the friend and patron of the kingdom of Granada. Ferdinand had had collections of moralizing tales (very much to the medieval taste) translated, as well as the Koran, Talmud, and Cabala. The conquests of Ferdinand III had placed Murcia (the home of ibn-Arabi) and Seville (the chief Islamic city after Cordoba) under Christian rule; El Sabio had himself been governor of Murcia. While in that city, the future sovereign had befriended al-Riqiti, a famous philosopher, and built a school for him where Muslims, Christians, and Jews could study together.

El Sabio was not only an encourager of tradition, he was also an author. His book on chess is the first account of the game in a European language. Chess had passed from India into Persia shortly before the Islamic conquest. Its Arabic name (derived originally from Sanskrit) was *al-shatranj*, which in Spanish became *ajedrex*. Some of the Arabic terms used have passed into modern use: the term "rook" for castle is said to

derive through the Spanish *roque* from the *rukh*, the fearsome monster met by Sindbad in *The Arabian Nights*. Other terms have, like the rules, evolved. El Sabio envisaged a larger number of squares than are used today; instead of the queen, he speaks of *alferza*, a word derived from *al-firzan*, the counselor; the bishop was *al-fila*, from the Arabic word for elephant. The later developments of the queen's powers were due to innovations introduced by two Spanish players, Lucena and Ruy López de Sigura, in the fifteenth and sixteenth centuries.

One book, translated into Latin and Spanish for El Sabio, shows once again that the wares that crossed the Spanish bridge came from farther afield than Greece or the Middle East. Originating in India, *Kalila and Dimna*, translated around 1250 as *Calina and Dygna*, takes its name from two jackals, one cunning, one naïvely good, whose discussion of how to gain the favor of the lion inserts fable inside fable, like Chinese box within Chinese box. The tale forms in sum one of the shrewdest commentaries on politics ever written. Some of the aphorisms, which delighted medieval man, still have punch today: "Three things a wise man will not do: tell secrets to women, experiment with poisons, or make friends with rulers." The political shrewdness had been acquired by the firsthand, if ultimately vain, experience of the author of the Arabic version, ibn-al-Muqaffa. Starting life as a Zoroastrian priest, he acquired with Islam his Arabic name, developed a rarely equaled Arabic style, and served an early Abbasid ruler whose wrath he ultimately incurred and who had him put to death.

To Arabs, *Kalila and Dimna* would come on any

وكان في الغدير سلحفاة بينها وبين البطتين مودة وصداقة فلما رأت غيض
ذلك لما نجا البطتان لوداع السلحفاء وقالتا السلام عليك قالتا ذا هبتان
عن هذا المكان لأجل نقصان الماء عنه قالت إنما بين نقصان الماء على مثلي الذي لا كان

السفينة لا تقدر على اليبس إلا الماء فإنما أتمنا أن نفقد أن على العيش حين حكمتما
بي معكما قالتا لها نعم قالت كيف السبيل إلى حملي قالتا إنا نأخذ بطرفي عود وتشبط
بوسطه وتطير بك في الحو إلا أنه إذا سمعنا الناس يتكلمون إلا أن نطيع لحذاها

short list of their prose classics. Yet ibn-al-Muqaffa's fables were not his own invention, as he admitted when he claimed that an Indian philosopher named Bidpai had composed them. He knew the original of his work in a Persian version, made before the coming of Islam. The original Sanskrit work named the two jackals Karatake and Damanaka and was intended as a cautionary mirror for dissolute princes. Because of its immense fame as an Arabic classic, and because of the profundity of its stories, numerous versions were made. It reached the Byzantine empire, for example, as early as the eleventh century in a Greek version dedicated to the emperor Alexius I Comnenus. An earlier version in Hebrew (which took great liberties with the text) was used as the basis for a Latin version by John of Capua, a baptized Jew, toward the end of the thirteenth century. But the most accurate version, and the only one to be made directly from the Arabic of ibn-al-Muqaffa, was the one made for El Sabio. The influence of *Kalila and Dimna* — more popularly known as "The Fables of Bidpai" — was to extend far into the coming centuries, culminating in the charming fables of Jean de La Fontaine, whose original genius nevertheless owed more than a trace to a repolished and Arabized Indian looking glass.

Fables were, of course, not the only literary form to be transmitted over the Spanish bridge. A major cultural revolution was constituted by the arrival, toward the end of the eleventh century, of a new poetry in Christian Europe. Rhymed and dedicated to love, it was first cultivated in southern France by the troubadours but reached its greatest height in the work of an Italian, Dante Alighieri, who was born in Florence

in 1265 and who died in Ravenna in 1321. This new poetry was long linked by literary critics with Arabic, whose verses had been rhymed since the time of Ignorance before Muhammad, and whose treatment of love anticipated in many ways that of the troubadours. In the nineteenth century, a time of European political power and Arab impotence, a critical reaction began to dispute this link, arguing that no documentary evidence existed to support it. But on this, as on the kindred question of how much Islamic mysticism influenced Christian mysticism, the last word perhaps belongs with Reynold A. Nicholson, a famous British Orientalist: "If in both cases direct evidence of transmission is frequently hard to obtain, the reason is that no written record can preserve the details of an intellectual communication carried on, over a long period of time, between two races living in daily intercourse with each other." That Spanish — or Romance — influenced Arabic poetry is certain, since in Andalus there developed an original verse form, the *muwashshah,* in which Arabic stanzas were capped by a stanza in the local language.

Dante's departure from the tradition of Vergil (the great Latin poet whom he takes for his guide to Hell and Purgatory) was in a direction already trod by the Arabs, whose poetry had always depended upon regular rhyme. Dante substitutes rhymed stanzas for Vergil's unrhymed hexameter and makes of his *Divina Commedia* an epic of the spirit rather than of arms and men. Much of the philosophy that informs his work derives from Islamic Spain. Modern scholarship has underlined his debt to ibn-Arabi in particular, though it is sometimes hard to see where affinity ends and borrowing begins. In Dante's *La Vita Nuova* he has a dream that a young man in a snow-white tunic is seated beside him in a pensive attitude. This repeats an ancient Sufi conception — of which ibn-Arabi has a variant — going back to a Saying of the Prophet: "I saw my Lord in a dream in the semblance of a most beautiful beardless youth." (Ibn-Arabi met "the youth steadfast in devotion" as he passed by the eastern corner of the Kaaba during a pilgrimage to Mecca.)

A Spanish critic, who claims that ibn-Arabi was influenced by Christian ideas, claims that Dante found in him "the general framework of his work, the poetic fiction of a mysterious journey to the regions beyond the grave, and its allegorical significance, the geometrical plans that schematise the architecture of the Inferno and the Paradiso, the general features that embellish the sublime drama, the plastic rendering of the glorious life of the elect, the beatific vision of the divine light and the ecstasy that accompanies it." For as another scholar, the Italian Bruno Nardi, has shown, Dante was not a pure Christian thinker but an eclectic philosopher who took his good where he found it, even from sources condemned by his Church. Dante's conception of the deity — that God is light and his rays are diffused and lose their intensity as they travel from the primal source; and that creation must be conceived as an ever-lessening emanation of divine light, realized not immediately by God, but through the medium of the celestial spheres — has some roots in Saint Augustine but more in ibn-Arabi. The image of the mirror, which Dante uses to explain the influence of superior beings on inferior, is in ibn-Arabi; so is the use of the circle and its center to represent the cosmos and its

divine principle. But the greatest affinities occur in the cult of platonic love. In his *Interpreter of Longings,* ibn-Arabi defended the platonic nature of his love for Nizam; Dante makes a similar defense in his *Banquet.*

Platonic love is one of the more mysterious links between Islam and Christendom. There is no justification for platonic love in the Koran, where sex is spoken of in the most practical terms and where pleasure and procreation are seen as its purposes. But ibn-Arabi took up a Saying much prized by Sufis in which Muhammad was reported to have said: "He who loves and remains chaste, and dies, is a martyr." Many Sufis left heroic examples of chastity within marriage, the woman becoming the companion and sister in the Way. Platonic love could also claim an origin in the practices of an Arabian tribe, the Beni 'Udra. The tribesmen were reputed to hold as an ideal the morbid perpetuation of unconsummated desire. This type of love — so similar to the unconsummated love of the troubadours — was sometimes known as 'Udri (after the tribe) and sometimes as Baghdadi, since it was elaborated in the Abbasid capital under the influence of Greek ideas.

Like other revolutionary concepts, platonic love began as an infiltrating idea, rose to a crescendo of conquering vigor, and declined into a figure of speech. In *The Ring of the Dove* the eleventh-century ibn-Hazm plays with the notion that love is the reunion of two separate halves — but makes it plain that sensual attraction is what makes the two halves recognize each other. By the fourteenth century, when the walls of the Alhambra were inscribed with the poems of ibn-Zamrak — making him the most lavishly published poet in history — this treatment of love had become a cliche.

Isen q̃ en vna abdat q̃ dizian gtin q̃ es en ssa de ya
bpt abia vn flo mercador τ abia su mugr muy
fermosa τ abia vn vezino pintor τ eña diudo della
Et dixol ella vn dia sy podrias fazer alguã cosa por q̃ te yo vnos
ق ese quañdo vrmeses am de nochẽ τ saldria aty syn q̃ me lla
mases tu por tal q̃ nos no sospechasen nĩ te oyesen dixol su
amygo yo te fare vna seña tan blanca cõmo lalus delaluna
Et fare en ella vnas pinturas τ qñdo las tus vezes saldras
al my diestra sera señal entre mj τ ty Et ploguela ael desto q̃l
dixo otoyolo lm su seyno della τ aptisolo τ encubriolo en su
corason

vema aella su amygo con aq̃lla señal τ veyalo ella ot
saua ael τ dixo assy vn põ Et despues fuese su amygo
pa el sey aptenle vnas casas q̃ abia de menester ot
fuese luego el seyno della adna mançeba q̃ tenja el pintor en
cuyo poder estaua la sauana otra su conosçente τ demandol
aq̃lla sauana τ ella diogela ot el fuese pa su señor de noche
τ luego q̃ ella vio lasauana de suso del auya q̃ eña su amygo
τ salio luego ael τ yuguse conella τ toñnose el seyno τ diola sa
uana ala mançeba del pintor

UBI METGENT MESSEM TERRE

UBI...

CIUITAS   UBI CALCATUM EST TORCULAR
EXTRA CIUITATE. ET EXIIT SANGUIS
DE TORCULARI USQUE AD FRENOS
EQUORUM

"There is no honey in the comb," a Spanish critic has written, "nor flowers around it; but some late bees clean and polish as never before the empty cells." But ibn-Arabi, who died only twenty-five years before Dante was born, packs the cells of his love poetry with royal jelly. His *Interpreter of Longings* is to platonic love what the Parthenon is to Hellenic architecture. Dante surely shows its transmitted effect in the passion for Beatrice, which is not only the scaffolding of his epic but its motive force.

These four individuals — Pope Sylvester II, Gerard of Cremona, Alfonso El Sabio, and Dante — stand out for qualities that made them different from the nameless masses who also used the Spanish bridge. The ordinary man is less excited by a new system of numerals or a new theory of love than he is by a new food or a new device to assist his business. While a pope, a translator, a king, and a poet were transmitting intellectual cargo to the West, men of whose biographies we know nothing were transmitting a material cargo of as great importance.

A chief feature of the medieval diet was its monotony. In introducing to Europe the cultivation of rice (whose name derives from Arabic by way of the Spanish *arroz*) and sugar cane, the Arabs greatly affected the European table. Rice was taken from Andalus to Pisa, where it was first grown only a generation before Columbus received the royal commission in Granada that was to lead to the discovery of America. Until the Arabs introduced sugar cane to southern Spain, Europeans had depended on honey to sweeten their food. With the discovery of America, Spain was to grow sugar cane in its new West Indian colonies, and the cultivation of it

in Europe was to die out. And although less important than rice or sugar, the pomegranate, which may have given its name to Granada, gave Europe a new flavor, particularly enjoyed in drinks.

Ordinary merchants wrought one big service, not only to their appetites, but to the needs of their more intellectual contemporaries. The diffusion of the knowledge acquired by men of the order of Sylvester II or Gerard of Cremona could never have accelerated in the way that it was to do in the Renaissance without printing, and printing could never have been invented without the use of paper. This material, as humble and as essential to modern civilization as water itself, was first introduced to Europe by the Arabs of Spain. The Arabs had come by it through an accident of war. In the mid-eighth century they were besieged in Samarkand, a city they had conquered earlier, by a force of Chinese. The garrison sallied from the city and took a number of Chinese prisoner, some of whom knew the art of papermaking. Having learned the process from their captives, the Arabs spread the manufacture of paper from one end of Islam to another, using flax or linen threads to make what El Sabio termed "cloth parchment." From such cities as Valencia and Toledo, where the manufacture was established in twelfth-century mills, the art of making paper passed into Italy and the rest of Europe. More than any other single invention, paper was to become the medium through which human wisdom, and sometimes human folly, were to reach the millions who could never have read books if they had continued to be written by hand on animal parchment. For the introduction of paper alone every writer and every reader owes a debt to Andalus.

VI
Reconquest

The reconquest of Andalus for Catholic Christendom is one of history's most surprising reverses. A no less surprising interval of more than two centuries divides the two phases in which it was effected. The first phase began with the collapse of the Cordoba caliphate in 1031 and was completed with the capture of Seville in 1248; all of Spain was by then in Christian hands except for the vassal sultanate of Granada. Then, after the reign of a score of sultans, the Catholic Sovereigns, Ferdinand of Aragon and Isabella of Castile, captured Granada in the first month of the year — 1492 — whose tenth month was to see the discovery of North America. Even during its active phases, the reconquest was far from being an orderly process. Triumph was soured by setback, unity by schism. And although the battles of the reconquest gave individual Spaniards opportunities for heroic gallantry, the spirit of intolerance that powered and poisoned the concluding phase produced a mood in which solemn obligations were forgotten and in which religious and racial bigotry ensured that the triumphs of the new Spain would be short-lived. The story of the reconquest is thus both the story of the Cid, Spain's greatest hero, and of the Inquisition, Spain's greatest shame. Its blend of glory and sorrow is typical of Spain.

The first phase of reconquest was the more difficult and the more heroic. Two royal couplings separated by a century signify the shift of power away from the Muslims. In 980, when the Moorish dictator-chamberlain Almanzor made one of his forays into the Christian lands to his north, the king of Navarre offered the conqueror his daughter. Almanzor accepted the gift with pleasure and made the girl his wife. The beautiful Christian princess embraced Islam and became one of the most religious women in the dictator's harem. The next century saw the enactment of a similar drama, but with an opposite cast. Alfonso VI, after the death of his queen, Constance of Burgundy, filled her place in his palace with Zaida, daughter of al-Mutamid, the poet-king of Seville. This time it was the Muslim woman who changed her religion. Zaida took a saint's name at baptism and bore the king his only son, Sancho, who might have succeeded to the throne had he not fallen in battle a year before his father's death. Since Islam normally punished apostasy with death, Zaida's cohabitation, as a Christian, with the conqueror of Toledo symbolized a dramatic change of fortune for the Arabs in Spain. From then on, even though there would be resounding victories, the Christian powers dominated and threatened; the Muslims of Andalus were overrun or enfiefed.

This change of fortune had its source in the disintegration of the caliphate. Before this happened, the formidable unity of Andalus was countered by no Christian equivalent, only by a jigsaw of feuding Christian states: from west to east, Galicia, León, Castile, Navarre, Aragon, and Barcelona. But once these feuding states saw a similar disarray among the Muslims, they were united in the vision of reconquest. And by this time, they were also in a position to enforce it. The Christians were no longer the weak, mixed populace that had proved so easy a conquest for the eighth-century Arabs. After sharing the peninsula with the Arabs for three centuries they knew the weaknesses of their neighbors as well as their strengths. As the Christian states began to nibble at

divided Andalus, they could also consolidate recovered territory with the formidable skills of the Mozarabs, whom the intolerance of North African invaders disposed to move north. A revived agriculture, a commerce in which Jews played as active a role on the Christian side as they had on the Arab, built a prospering base for the operation of reconquest. Religious passion provided a powerful motive. Although a mirror emotion to that of the Arabs, the Catholic faith was embodied in a hierarchy whose love for Christ and hatred of non-Christians were inextricably blended.

Along with an intense religious faith, the Spanish Christians shared other characteristics with the Muslims. The diverse passions of amour propre and devotion to one's family group inclined the Spaniards as much as the Moors to factionalism. Thus, driven alternately by idealism and anarchic egoism, the reconquest was to pursue a zigzag rather than a straightforward course. Even while it was being most energetically advanced, the Spaniards were as often fighting one another as the Moors. Repeatedly, national unity would dissolve just as it had seemed assured.

The first major figure of the reconquest was Ferdinand I. He managed to unite Galicia, León, and Castile under his rule in 1037, just as the caliphate had dissolved into a medley of temptingly disunited states. Ferdinand chose northern Portugal for his first attacks, freeing the area of the Tagus. By his death in 1065, he had made Seville, Badajoz, Toledo, and Saragossa his tributaries, even though they still had Muslim kings. These paid tribute, part from an inability to refuse, part from the private hope each nursed of reuniting Andalus and reversing the tide. While Ferdinand was fighting in the west and south, the king of Aragon was eroding the Muslims' territories in the rich Ebro plain.

Yet typically Ferdinand left a will that undid much of his achievements. Having consolidated Galicia, León, and Castile into one Christian state, he proceeded to dissolve the unity by bequeathing the kingdoms to three separate sons. The proper pride of these three ensured civil wars that enabled Seville, the leading Arab state, to regain some of its power. Al-Mutamid, who briefly regained prestigious Cordoba, wrote as though he had won some disdainful beauty: "I have won at the first onset the hand of the lovely Cordoba: that brave Amazon who with sword and spear repelled all those who sought her in marriage." And although the anarchy was to be resolved when the son who had inherited León gained possession of Galicia and Castile as well, it illustrates the feuding pattern that complicated a general sense of national mission. And that the Spaniards could be as factious as the Muslims was soon shown by the relations between this king, Alfonso VI, and the Cid, not only Spain's greatest hero, but history's most outstanding free-lance soldier.

Alfonso, the sixth Spanish king to bear that name, is also the first Alfonso to be more than a shadowy figure of disputed dates. Reigning from 1065 until his death in 1109, he was an aggressive warrior-king whose prowess was feared and whose word was trusted by all his foes. He was also a Janus figure, as befitted the ruler of a geographical bridge between cultures. At one end, and under the influence of his Burgundian wife, he encouraged the importation of French military, ecclesiastical, and cultural ideas; by substituting the Latin Mass for the Gothic liturgy of Saint Isidore of Seville, he integrated Spanish Catholicism into that of Europe as a whole. Spain, under Alfonso, became for the first time an articulate part of crusading Europe, although it was fighting the Muslims at home and not in Palestine. At the other end, Alfonso's standard of values remained similar to that of the Arabs, with whom as allies, friends, or vassals he remained on close social terms. (Of the ruler of Toledo he once said, "He is a gentleman, albeit a Moor.") He was the suzerain of al-Mutamid of Seville, then the chief Arab kingdom. On one occasion ibn-Ammar, the Arab king's friend, fellow poet, and prime minister, saved his city from conquest by siege through a strategem that depended on shrewd knowledge of Alfonso's impetuous yet chivalrous nature.

"Knowing the king's fondness for chess," in the words of the noted Arabist Reinhart Dozy, "he ordered a chess-board to be made of workmanship so exquisite that no king possessed its equal. The men were of ebony and sandal-wood inlaid with gold. Provided with this work of art, he visited, under some pretext, Alfonso's camp, and was courteously received." Once Alfonso saw the chess set, his heart desired it. A game was arranged against a wager. If the king won, he would keep the set; if ibn-Ammar won, he would be allowed one boon. The Arab won and at once asked him to raise the siege of Seville. Bound by his oath, Alfonso withdrew. This did not, however, prevent him from doubling the tribute or pushing on as far south as Tarifa where he plunged his horse into the sea, claiming, rather prematurely, to have reconquered the utmost land of Spain.

With the Arab king of Toledo, to whom Alfonso was bound by friendship, new difficulties of principle arose. Only when a revolt dislodged the king did Alfonso feel liberated from any obligations not to attack the city. His capture of Toledo in 1085 marked as decisive a strategic shift as his marriage to al-Mutamid's daughter marked a moral shift. Toledo, the old Visigothic capital, was the strategic shield of Islamic Andalus.

The extent of Alfonso's triumphs proved a danger to himself and the Christian cause. The loss of Toledo brought the squabbling Muslims to their senses. Even al-Mutamid agreed to seek North African help. The year after the loss of Toledo, Almoravide warriors surged across the straits from Morocco and inflicted a calamitous defeat on Alfonso's forces near Badajoz, on the Guadiana River in southwest Spain.

Fortunately for Alfonso, various factors prevented the Almoravide emperor, ibn-Tashfin, from exploiting his victory. Preoccupied with troubles at home, he at once withdrew to Africa. Although he returned four years later, he was less eager to wage holy war than to suppress the *taifa* kings and add verdant Andalus to his arid empire. Although Alfonso died saddened by the death of his half-Arab son, he knew that his crusading work would not be undone. And although he was Spain's most redoubtable soldier-king, Alfonso VI was nonetheless the only Spanish sovereign to be eclipsed in his own lifetime by a subject noble.

Rodrigo (or Ruy) Díaz de Bivar is known to legend and history as the Cid. (This title came from the Arabic word *sayyid*, originally meaning "lord," nowadays the Arab equivalent of "mister.") No other figure in

Alfonso VII of León and Castile is shown (left) on the way to his coronation, where the somewhat empty title of emperor was conferred upon him. Alfonso helped slow the pace of reconquest first by raiding Andalus, bringing in the Almohades, and then by splitting his realm between his sons, Sancho and Ferdinand. In the picture at right, Alfonso (far right) is granting a charter to a bishop (center) while Sancho and Ferdinand look on (left).

European military history entered ballad and heroic tale so swiftly or stayed there so long: as the paragon of Christian knighthood, he inspired poets from the twelfth century to the seventeenth. The result of his astonishing fame was the creation of a legendary icon — the Perfect One, the Born in a Happy Hour — that tempted at least one scholar to deny his historical existence. Modern research makes it certain that the Cid did exist, and even if it peels away much of the fabulous, what it leaves is vivid enough.

The Cid, probably born at Bivar, a village near Burgos, was a prominent noble at the court of the Ferdinand I who launched the reconquest. On Ferdinand's death he fought for a while in the cause of his son Sancho II, to whom the king had bequeathed Castile. After Sancho was worsted, the Cid recognized his victorious brother, Alfonso VI, as king. Alfonso showed his initial approval of his subject by marrying him to his own kinswoman, Ximena, and then sending him to Seville to collect the tribute. Two ensuing exploits aroused first the jealousy, then the anger of the king. In an inter-Arab war between Seville and Granada the Cid routed some Castilian knights who were aiding Granada; he next attacked Toledo, although that city was still ruled by Alfonso's Arab ally. As a result, in 1081, just four years before Alfonso took Toledo himself, the Cid was exiled from Castile for the first time. Six heroic years were consumed in free-lance campaigns under banners sometimes Christian, other times Muslim.

This first exile was followed by a two-year return to apparent royal favor — but not trust. Alfonso showed his continuing suspicions of his powerful vassal by suddenly confiscating his property and jailing his wife and children. Once again the Cid rode into exile. This time he placed his sword at the disposal of the Muslim king of Saragossa, at war with the Christians of Catalonia. The Cid's chivalrous treatment of Catalan war prisoners led to the marriage of his daughter to the future count of Barcelona.

The invasion of the Almoravides forced all Christians back on the same side, and the Cid once more fought alongside Alfonso. But the king remained obdurate, and soon the Cid was banished from Castile for his third period of exile. For the first time rancor seems to have soured his actions, and he began to ravage the territory of his native land. He also carved out a fiefdom for himself. Appointed commander in chief of a largely Muslim army, he bolstered the authority of the Arab king of Valencia, then the richest city on the peninsula. A revolt against this king gave the Cid his chance to seize Valencia for himself. His possession of this key point on the east coast from 1094 to his death in 1099 proved a fortunate accident for Christian Spain, for the Almoravide army was thereby prevented from advancing up the coastal plain to retake the rich Ebro valley from the Christians. After his death, his valiant widow, Ximena, carried on for three years until 1102, when Alfonso found the city's position untenable. Orders were given to evacuate. From the burning city the Cid's body was carried to burial in Burgos.

His royal master, kinsman, ally, and opponent survived the Cid by ten years. Then, once again, the problem of the succession produced anarchy. Alfonso had left the throne to his daughter, Urraca, and her infant son by the king of Aragon. (The marriage had broken up thanks to the king's domineering temper and Urraca's promiscuity.) A period of strife between Castile and Aragon ended only with Urraca's death in 1126. Luckily for the Christians, this period of squabbling coincided with the decadence of Almoravide power. While Castile was too busy to profit, Aragon's king captured Saragossa in 1118 and pushed south as far as Granada, bringing back some fourteen thousand Mozarabs to populate and develop the reconquered land south of the Ebro.

A new southward surge — by Alfonso VII, who in 1144 temporarily occupied Cordoba — provoked the intervention of the Almohades, much as the capture of Toledo had provoked that of the Almoravides. When Alfonso died in 1157, he was buried as an emperor. But the title was hollow. It belonged to him personally and not to his state; neither was it transmitted to his heirs, for once again a royal will plunged Spain into chaos. Alfonso left his empire to his sons, Sancho and Ferdinand, kings respectively of Castile and León. After a period of uncertainty, his grandson Alfonso VIII emerged as master of Castile. But Spain endured another sixty anarchic years during which the Almohades substantially restored the fabric of Andalus, though they could not expand its frontiers. At first their Berber and Negro soldiers made them militarily more powerful than the Spaniards, as was shown when they crushingly defeated Alfonso VIII at Alarcos, a little to the west of the modern Ciudad Real. Twenty-five thousand Spaniards are said to have been killed or wounded. Nor was Castile in a state of peace with its Christian neighbors León and Navarre. Not until the beginning of the thirteenth century was something approaching a united Spain ready to take its revenge and open the way to

further reconquest. In 1212, two years before his death, Alfonso VIII decisively defeated the Moors at the battle of Las Navas de Tolosa.

Although Alfonso's death and that of the last Almohade emperor, Yusuf II, occurred within two years of each other, they left very different societies behind them. Whereas the death of Yusuf left Andalus split into such warring, vulnerable statelets as Valencia, Murcia, and Granada, Alfonso's successor Ferdinand III was able in 1230 finally to unite León with Castile and make of this larger Castilian kingdom not only the battle-ax of reconquest, but also its brains. (Aragon, the kingdom to the east of the Iberian range, was more preoccupied with events in the south of France, though Aragonese troops captured the Balearic Islands as well as substantial territory on the east coast of Spain itself.) By 1236 Ferdinand had captured Cordoba and by 1248 Seville. He had thus reduced the Muslim holding in the peninsula to Granada, a tiny sultanate containing the one fertile valley, the Vega, and a chain of ports west to Cadiz. Its Nasrid sultans recognized the overlordship of Castile and as such attended the Cortes, or parliament, on demand. The first sultan, who founded the Alhambra, displayed his humiliating dependency when he agreed to supply soldiers to help the king of Castile reduce Muslim Seville.

Ferdinand III died in 1252, before he could carry out the next step in his policy — the conquest, not of Granada, which he probably saw as a convenient reservation for the country's Muslims, but of North Africa, which, as a potential breeding ground of fierce invaders, continued to threaten Christian Spain. Ferdinand's death ended the first phase of the reconquest and left

Granada to maintain, for more than two centuries, the phantom of Arab glory. The reasons why it was allowed to do so lay in Castile, since Aragon was by now cut off from physical contact with the Moors by Castilian territory. The Islamic presence of Granada by this time seemed remote and unthreatening, even to Castile. Since all Christians had left the sultan's kingdom, which instead was swollen with Muslim refugees from the north, religious friction was largely absent. Nor were the Granadans dangerous, for while they still recruited African soldiers for the sultan's army, they had learned the perils of invoking Berber aid, even though no Berber force existed after the extinction of the Almohades. Castile, divided by dynastic quarrels, experienced the turbulence of a baronial class similar to that which in England caused the Plantaganet monarchy to founder. Such kings as Alfonso El Sabio tried in vain to impose absolute rule, but self-willed barons revolted against these attempts at control and sometimes even aided Granada in its periodic spats with Castile. Granada thus remained yet another piece on the chessboard of small, independent states that made up medieval Spain.

The final reconquest of all Spain was to be achieved after the union of Castile with Aragon, just as the first phase had been completed after the union of Castile with León. This union resulted from the marriage of Isabella of Castile to Ferdinand II of Aragon at Valladolid on October 19, 1469. The terms of their marriage contract came into force in 1474, when Isabella was declared queen of Castile and León. Isabella henceforth remained sovereign in Castile — the senior half of the kingdom to which her power-hungry husband

also had a claim — but the royal pair exercised justice conjointly when they were together or independently when they were apart.

Isabella was the dominant partner and her generous and generally clear-sighted nature was in turn dominated by a ravening piety that saw in the acceptance of diversity a tolerance of sin, not a recipe for cultural wealth. But it would be wrong to attribute Isabella's burning resolution to conquer Granada — one of two great causes for which she was prepared to part with her jewels — merely to bigotry, though bigot by modern standards she certainly was. Political considerations also prompted her policy. The fifteenth century was marked in the Mediterranean by the dramatic rise of the house of Osman, the last great Muslim dynasty. From a small base in what is now western Turkey, these border warriors had conquered the Balkans and by storming Constantinople in 1453 had established the Ottoman sultan as heir to the Caesars, if not the caliphs. Ottoman naval power reached west across the Mediterranean to threaten North Africa and Spain.

In themselves, their fellow Muslims of Granada were no threat. A century earlier one of the greatest Arab geniuses, ibn-Khaldun, had summed them up in his pioneer work on the philosophy of history: "These Arabs of Spain have lost the spirit of solidarity and mutual assistance which produce political power. They only retain their family trees. . . . Subjected by force and sated with humiliations, they imagine that with lineage and a post in the government one can easily conquer a kingdom and govern men." Middle-class, not particularly luxurious, the citizens of the last Muslim state in western Europe lived orderly lives, were orthodox in their religious beliefs, paid their taxes regularly, had a sound currency, and passed the hot summers in their villas in the luxuriant Vega. Their wives, on the short side and given to being stout, were laden with jewels. "On Fridays," says another Arab writer, "in the mosques, they are like full blown flowers beneath gentle breezes in a meadow."

Yet as this society awaited its enemies' final and inevitable pounce, there was a curious reversion to Eastern influences. In the first period, when the Alhambra was abuilding, it might have seemed as though a cultural symbiosis would eventually swallow this Islamic enclave. A contemporary Arab historian records that the turban was rarely worn, and certainly not by the king, as the sultan preferred to be called.

The sultan and his troops usually adopt the dress of their Christian neighbours; they have the same arms, the same cloaks, those of scarlet like the others. Their flags are the same, their saddles and their way of making war with shields and long lances for throwing. They have no acquaintance with the maces and bows of the Arabs; rather they employ Christian bows when besieging cities, and their infantry use them in military expeditions.

But as the end drew nearer, the Granadans had reverted to Arab titles and to an Arab style in war, using simple armor, gilt helmets, leather shields, and, for the cavalry, light lances. As any hopes of an Islamic counterattack faded and as Granada became more isolated, it became more defiantly different. The Spanish historian Leopoldo Torres Balbás writes:

A Castilian of the 13th or 14th century who visited for the first time a city of Muslim Spain must have been impressed by the gay polychromy of the minarets and external walls of many buildings; a polychromy achieved through the combination of diverse materials, by ceramics and painting. . . . Castile with its sterilised ex-Moorish cities was by contrast grey: Nasrid Granada stood out, unique, coloured, luminous against the green pedestal of its plain, the Vega.

And at the heart of Granada was the Alhambra which:

By permission of the judge of beauty
Remits the tax in two coins:
For if, at dawn, in the hands of the west wind
It drops drachmas of light, which would be ample,
In the thicket, among the tree-trunks,
It bestows doubloons of sun-gold, which bedeck it.

The final clash between these contrasted societies began in 1481, when the nineteenth sultan foolishly seized a castle belonging to Castile. The eleven years of war that followed was no series of Castilian walkovers. Ferdinand was defeated at Loja, southeast of Granada, and chased as far as Cordoba; he was next defeated near Malaga. But the Arabs were unfortunate in Boabdil, their final sultan, nor had they lost with time their tendency to split into factions. A Spanish victory of 1483 had left Boabdil temporarily in Castilian hands, giving his captors the chance to study his character. They learned that he was motivated solely by the desire to maintain his city and palace, at whatever cost to his fellow Muslims. With such skillful advisers as the duke of Cadiz, the Catholic Sovereigns managed to split their enemies into the diminishing followers of Boabdil and a majority who followed his tough, resourceful uncle, al-Zaghal. The division of their enemies facilitated the Spaniards' campaigns. Between 1483 and 1487

The taking of Granada was both a diplomatic and a military victory, resulting equally as much from Ferdinand's remarkable skill at setting the Muslim leaders at one another's throats as it did from the prowess of his men-at-arms. It was also a drawn-out affair, beginning in 1482, when a small contingent of Spanish Christians stormed the fortified walls of the Nasrid town of Alhama, then opened the gates to their main force. The Muslims retaliated with a siege, but withdrew when reinforcements were sent from the north. Scenes of the fighting at Alhama (below) and Granada (right) are depicted on a series of choir stalls that were carved for the cathedral at Toledo in 1495.

the Spaniards captured ten of the remaining Muslim cities, culminating in Malaga. The final storming of the key fortress of Baza led to the surrender of al-Zaghal. Only Granada and Boabdil remained to be subdued. The Catholic Sovereigns prepared themselves for a siege. The first improvised royal camp — in the farm of Gozco to the southeast of Granada — was destroyed by fire. A regular Roman-style siege city was then constructed some seven miles from Granada and named Santa Fé. Its ditches and solid turreted walls symbolized the determination of Isabella and her husband to close once and for all the Muslim chapter of Spain's history. This determination also delayed for a time the turning of a new chapter in human history: the discovery of the New World.

Christopher Columbus, the Genoese mapmaker, seafarer, and practical scientist, had argued since 1479 that by sailing toward the setting sun it would be possible for Europeans to reach the Indies or Japan. To prove his point he needed a sponsor. Since he was married to a cousin of the archbishop of Lisbon, he pinned his first hopes on the king of Portugal, but in these he was deceived. He then concluded that resurgent Spain was his most likely ally. Thanks to his friendship with a Spanish nobleman, the count of Medina Celi, the seafarer was summoned to the court of Isabella and Ferdinand at Cordoba. But 1486 was a bad year in which to expound his enticing but seemingly chimerical vision. All the ardor of the royal couple was devoted to the war; the Catholic Sovereigns had put off consideration of other questions until the reconquest was accomplished.

Thus Columbus, driven by a bolder dream than the

reduction of one last unconforming enclave, had to kick his heels for a better moment. Supported by Cardinal Pedro González de Mendoza, the third power in Spain, he trailed the court all around the embattled peninsula. According to one tradition, he took part in the siege of Malaga in 1487. But though treated with respect as an officer in the royal service, though given doles of money and encouraging words, Columbus was middle-aged in an epoch when time eroded health and vigor early, cruelly. He thought in desperation of trying Portugal once again, of England and France. On learning that the council of Salamanca, appointed to consider his proposals, had pronounced them "vain, impracticable, and resting on grounds too weak to merit the support of the government," he decided to take up what seemed a promising offer from the somewhat unreliable King Charles VIII of France.

Columbus left the court for Huelva, a small port near Cadiz. On his way he visited one of his staunchest supporters, Juan Pérez, guardian of a nearby convent and a former confessor to the queen. Pérez immediately left for Santa Fé, where the royal couple was preparing for the final assault on Granada. In his advocacy of Columbus, Pérez was joined by other leading personalities who were similarly convinced. An invitation from the Catholic Sovereigns, backed by money for his expenses, was at once sent to Columbus. Thus by one of history's less ordinary coincidences the man destined to discover a new world arrived near Granada, the last beautiful expression of a culture nearly eight centuries old, just as it was to pass into the hands of Isabella and Ferdinand. The season in which Boabdil, last of the Nasrid rulers of Granada, decided to resist no longer

Boabdil, whose great sword (below) became a prize of war, is shown in bas-relief (left) in the Royal Chapel surrendering Granada. According to a Spanish account, the cross entered Granada by one gate as the Koran left it by another, and the Te Deum resounded within walls still echoing with Allah Akbar ("God is most great"). The vanquished Nasrid was given an estate in Alpujarras, a mountainous area between the Sierra Nevada and the Mediterranean Sea, but he soon crossed the Strait of Gibraltar to Fez, where he died c. 1533.

and surrender was also to be the season of hope for the idea-tormented sailor.

Columbus himself refers to the surrender on the first page of his *Diario de las Derrotas y Caminos:*

> After Your Highnesses ended the war of the Moors who reigned in Europe, and finished the war of the great city of Granada, where this present year [1492] on the 2nd January I saw the royal banners of Your Highnesses planted by force of arms on the towers of the Alhambra, which is the fortress of the said city, I saw the Moorish king issue from the gates of the said city, and kiss the royal hands of Your Highnesses. . . .

The Alhambra was taken by the threat of force; it was not stormed. Negotiations on the terms of surrender had gone on during the last weeks of 1491, and as the new year dawned all was set for a final scene, one that would be magnificent and unstained by blood.

On the morning of January 2, 1492, the Catholic Sovereigns and their court discarded the mourning that had been put on for the Portuguese husband of Princess Isabella, killed in a riding accident. In most sumptuous attire the royal procession moved from Santa Fé to a place a little more than a mile from Granada, where Ferdinand took up his position by the banks of the Genil. A private letter written by an eyewitness to the bishop of León only six days after the event preserves the scene. With the royal banners and the cross of Christ plainly visible on the red walls of the Alhambra:

> . . . the Moorish king with about eighty or a hundred on horseback very well dressed went forth to kiss the hand of their Highnesses. Whom they received with much love and courtesy and there they handed over

to him his son, who had been a hostage from the time of his capture, and as they stood there there came about four hundred captives, of those who were in the enclosure, with the cross and a solemn procession singing the *Te Deum Laudamus,* and their highnesses dismounted to adore the Cross to the accompaniment of the tears and reverential devotion of the crowd, not least of the Cardinal and Master of Santiago and the Duke of Cadiz and all the other grandees and gentlemen and people who stood there, and there was no one who did not weep abundantly with pleasure giving thanks to Our Lord for what they saw, for they could not keep back the tears; and the Moorish King and the Moors who were with him for their part could not disguise the sadness and pain they felt for the joy of the Christians, and certainly with much reason on account of their loss, for Granada is the most distinguished and chief thing in the world, both in greatness and in strength as also in richness of dwelling places, for Seville is but a straw hut compared to the Alhambra. . . . Your lordship must believe that it was the most notable and blessed day that there ever was in Spain.

For Columbus it was certainly a blessed day, removing as it did the obstacle of royal preoccupation. Even so Ferdinand's cold disbelief in the worth of the undertaking imposed one last setback. But this was overcome when Columbus was but a few leagues from Granada by the more imaginative Isabella's act of faith: "I will assume the undertaking, for my own crown of Castile, and am ready to pawn my jewels to defray the expenses of it, if the funds in the treasury shall be found inadequate." Recalled once again to the royal

An odd offshoot of the completion of the reconquest was the discovery of the New World. While all their energies — and funds — were devoted to fighting the Muslims, the Catholic Sovereigns had no time for other pursuits. Once the war was won, however, they were free to take on other endeavors. Thus Columbus was granted the royal patronage he had sought for so long. With three ships similar to the one at right provided by the Crown, he departed on his fateful voyage. His landfall is celebrated in the contemporary print (left) showing him setting foot on an idealized shore while Ferdinand directs the venture from across an Atlantic of duckpond proportions.

court, which was still at Santa Fé, Columbus was appointed on April 17, 1492, "admiral, viceroy and governor general of all such islands and continents as he should discover in the western ocean. . . ." Columbus left Granada (which the royal couple had by then ceremonially entered) on May 12 and on August 3, 1492, in Prescott's words, "the intrepid navigator, bidding adieu to the Old World, launched forth on that unfathomed waste of waters where no sail had been ever spread before."

Boabdil, the last Moorish king, had embarked with his retinue on a sadder journey. As the royal party moved south toward exile in North Africa they reached a rocky eminence which gave a last view of the delectable city. Boabdil reined in his horse and surveying for the last time the Alhambra and the green valley that spread below he burst into tears. "You do well," said his unsympathetic mother, "to weep like a woman for what you could not defend like a man." While the sultana thought in terms of personal loss, Boabdil may have been weeping for the Spain to which, as much as his victors, he belonged.

The sultan had haggled closely over the conditions for surrender: the Catholic Sovereigns had agreed to terms which if honored would safeguard the interests of Boabdil's subjects and religion. While the persons and property of all Moors wishing to remain were completely guaranteed, the freedom of those who wished to leave to take their movable possessions with them was explicitly defined. All prisoners were to be freed. Taxes were to be no higher than those paid to the sultan. The Islamic religion and the law derived from it were to be faithfully preserved.

But the Catholic Sovereigns were animated by a spirit different from that which had inspired the eighth-century Arabs to give similar terms to Christians, and honor them. There was a brief attempt at reconciliation between the two cultures. Granada's Archbishop Talavera, while wishing to make conversions, wished to do so gently. He distributed among the priests who moved into Granada a volume entitled *Arte Para Saber Ligeramenta la Lengua Arábiga,* or "Arabic Without Tears." But this approach was thought too tepid. Almost at once Cardinal Jiménez de Cisnéros, a churchman of a different temper, was sent to stiffen Talavera. At the cardinal's instigation, the letter and spirit of the terms under which Granada had surrendered were broken. Arabic was anathematized as "the rude language of an heretical and despised race," while a public bonfire of 80,000 Arabic volumes disgraced Granada. A policy of enforced conversion was put into effect.

Whereas Islam had from its inception recognized that it enjoyed no monopoly of divine revelation, the faith of Isabella and Ferdinand acknowledged no validity in the religious notions of Jews and Muslims. Judaism and Islam were now to suffer full-scale persecution. The burning of books was to be followed by the burning of bodies.

The Jews suffered first, perhaps because they seemed theologically more objectionable than the Muslims (who were regarded as heretics) and because they were more envied, being richer. As early as 1391, Christian Spaniards had shown their hatred for Jews. Starting in the wealthy Juderia of Seville, anti-Jewish outbursts had erupted from the Pyrenees to the Balearic Islands. A Jewish historian has written:

Except in Granada and Portugal, hardly a single community was spared. The solitary way of escape from death lay through baptism. For the only time, perhaps in the whole of their long history, the morale of the Jews broke. Elsewhere, it had only been a small and weak remnant which saved its life by apostasy. . . . A very large proportion of the Jews, when offered the alternative of baptism or death, chose the former.

But this had solved the problem neither for the Jews nor for the Spaniards who wished to create a homogeneous state.

The New Christians — Marranos, or "swine," as they were known colloquially — soon formed a large and uneasy segment of Spanish society. Though some New Christians achieved high positions in Church and State, though many intermarried with Spaniards, most conversions made to escape the sword lacked conviction; many Marranos continued to observe the Jewish law in secret. To deal with this problem — a problem that the Spanish Christians had themselves created — negotiations were conducted by Cardinal Rodrigo Borgia (later Pope Alexander VI) with Pope Sixtus IV for the establishment in Castile of an Inquisition under royal, not ecclesiastical, authority to deal with the problem of converted Jews.

This new Inquisition started work in Seville in 1480 with such ruthlessness that the converted Jews began to flee en masse and the pope himself tried to arrest the process. In the same year, Isabella decided to expel all unconverted Jews from reconquered Andalusia. A movement of persecution developed that was to reach its climax after the fall of Granada: in 1483 Jews were expelled from the dioceses of Seville and Cordoba;

in 1486 all young Jews had to leave Burgos; in 1490 it was forbidden for any Jew to spend the night in Bilbao. In Aragon, where Ferdinand was anxious to take similar steps, there was popular resistance. In 1485 Ferdinand's inquisitor was assassinated in the cathedral at Saragossa — though this only gave new pretexts for persecution. The appointment of the sinister Torquemada as inquisitor general for Castile in 1483 must have played its part in the decision taken in March, 1492 — even earlier than the decision to back Columbus — to expel all unconverted Jews from Spain. Thereafter the Inquisition busied itself with those who had been baptized. Up to the eighteenth century, converted Jews provided the Inquisition's chief clients in Portugal and Spain.

The Muslims were soon to suffer an analogous fate. Anger at the burning of their religious books and indignation at attempts to convert them by force prompted a revolt that in turn served as pretext for an order on February 12, 1502 under which all unbaptized Moors were expelled from what had been the kingdom of Castile. Those who accepted baptism were to suffer a similar fate to that of the Jews, though their nickname was Moriscos, not Marranos. A series of measures against the Moriscos made their life more and more difficult. For example, a decree in 1525 forbade them to use Arab names or wear jewelry with Arab motifs; they were also forbidden to make marriage contracts in their traditional way. A further decree, in 1556, enforced the use of Castilian and imposed severe penalties on the use of Arabic.

Even those Moriscos who genuinely tried to comply with these enactments remained second-class citizens,

Although the Spanish Inquisition was originally set up to seek out converted Jews who were relapsing, it was soon extended to investigating Muslims and then Catholic Spaniards as well, in an attempt to impose a rigid orthodoxy upon the populace. With its endless processions of victims who had been accused — often anonymously — of heresy, its public courts, and its savage penalties, the Inquisition has won for itself a richly deserved and enduring reputation for infamy.

for to requirements of creedal exactitude (constantly under scrutiny by prying inquisitors) were added those of racial purity. No Morisco could enter a seminary or serve in the army or work in the legal profession, since admission was reserved for those who could demonstrate *limpieza de sangre,* "purity of blood" — or in other words prove that they derived from families untainted by Judaism, Islam, or heresy. Humiliations were wide-ranging. A decree of 1567 not only forbade Moriscos to own arms, but also ordered the physical destruction of all Moorish baths. The further revolts that these measures inspired further divided the Morisco population from the Christian. Measures by which the Moriscos of Granada were dispersed in the north in general failed to promote assimilation. The Moriscos became a discontented element in an impoverished society. By the reign of Philip III, the beggar, the vagabond, the picaro, rogues living by their wits, constantly on the move, defeated one day, triumphant the next, were the symbols of Castile.

In a state of economic stagnation — with less silver now coming from America and taxes at home yielding less — the government took the demagogic decision to expel all identifiable Moriscos, whether they were sincere Christians or not. The decision was probably popular. The Moriscos had the reputation of working too hard, spending too little, and breeding too fast. Those landlords who had no Morisco laborers were jealous of those who had. Those Spaniards who claimed to put country first argued that Moriscos living near the coast constituted a security risk; if they did not conspire with the Turks for reasons of religion they might well conspire with France (Spain's new chief enemy) for money. Summary decrees of 1609 and 1610 required the Moriscos of Castile, Valencia, Catalonia, and Aragon to leave Spain forthwith. In all, just under 300,000 — or about half the contemporary population of Scotland — appear to have been expelled. In many areas of Spain they left deserted fields; in North Africa many found hostility, on the grounds that they were Christians at heart.

Thus the capture of the Alhambra in a golden moment of Spanish history meant that Christian Spain was not to produce its own equivalent of the Cordoba caliphate. With the expulsion of the Jews, who understood medicine and commerce, and of the Moors and Moriscos, who were skilled in agriculture and crafts, Spain became a closed society on the defensive in impossible wars. Battling to ward off the Turks with one hand and with the other to maintain the New World against all comers, the Spanish monarchs also fought their own people, restricting commerce with America to the city of Seville (for the better supervision of taxation) and levying counterproductive imposts on every stage of the productive process.

The Arabs were thus not only expelled but in a sense revenged. As swordsman and executioner of the Counter-Reformation, Spain became the living proof that intolerance brought a nation low. The seventeenth century, which elsewhere in Europe saw an unprecedented awakening of the mind, saw in Spain and Portugal its two most beggarly nations. By intruding his Renaissance palace next to the delicate structure of the Alhambra, Charles V, grandson of Ferdinand and Isabella, left a symbol of the ponderous regime that would conduct his country into stagnant centuries.

The baptism of the Moors is shown in bas-relief in Granada's Royal Chapel. Exile and death were the alternatives to baptism, but even receiving that sacrament did not ease the status of the convert. He continued to be in a despised and discriminated-against minority. Of those who chose exile, many settled along the coast of North Africa and became corsairs, posing a serious threat to Spanish ships.

VII

The Afterglow

It was a disastrous event, even though they say the opposite in the schools. An admirable civilization and a poetry, architecture, and delicacy unique in the world — all were lost, to give way to an impoverished, cowed town, a wasteland populated by the worst bourgeoisie in Spain today." Such was the judgment of Spain's twentieth-century poet, Federico García Lorca, on the concluding event in the reconquest of Andalus. The fact that he was himself from Granada, Lorca said, gave him "a sympathetic understanding of those who are persecuted — of the gypsy, the negro, the Jew, of the Moor which all granadinos carry inside them." In 1936, perhaps for saying just such things, Lorca was murdered, along with many ordinary Granadans, by the heirs of the reconquerors whom he deplored.

Lorca was correct in saying that another view of the reconquest was general in Spanish schools. There it was taught that the capture of Granada marked a glorious victory for Spanish arms against an alien threat. This view went back to the time of Ferdinand and Isabella. "The most high, most Catholic, and most powerful lords, Don Fernando and Doña Isabel, our King and Queen, conquered by force of arms this Kingdom and city of Granada, which, after their highnesses had besieged it in person for a considerable time, was surrendered to them by the Moorish King . . . together with its Alhambra and other fortresses, on the 2nd day of January, 1492." So reads the inscription in Gothic letters set up over a cistern by Don Iñigo López de Mendoza, count of Tendilla, appointed by his sovereigns as custodian. Granada and the Alhambra were seen as wondrous prizes, not symbols of a culture that merited respect and preservation.

During the ensuing three centuries of Spanish rule, Granada, along with other formerly Islamic cities, suffered either cultural and economic sterilization or depredation. Far from being repented, Cardinal Jiménez's "conversion" of the Moors was to be glorified in an altar panel in the Royal Chapel annexed to Granada's cathedral. Far from preserving the fabric of Cordoba's Great Mosque, Charles V, grandson of Ferdinand and Isabella, intruded an incongruous cathedral in the middle of its cool, treelike aisles. Since Granada symbolized the final bulwark of Arab Spain, the town was deliberately transformed. A desire first to Christianize, then modernize, erased much of its Islamic character from the last capital of Andalus. A cathedral replaced the mosque; the Old Mosque quarter, which survived as late as the nineteenth century, was then torn down to make way for a gridiron of streets, lit, to their residents' pride, by electricity.

Fortunately the Alhambra's prestige as a prize of war preserved it from being pulled down or turned into a convent. Ferdinand and Isabella contented themselves with "purging" the Old Mosque and conserving it as a Christian chapel. (It had been the site of the assassination of the sultan who built the Gate of Justice.) Both Charles V and his son Philip II (at one time the husband of England's Mary Tudor) spent generously in adapting the Alhambra for the use of the Christian court and courtiers. The room now known as the Queen's Dressing Room was modernized and painted in arabesque by Charles; reputedly, perfumes were wafted through the holes in a marble slab in one corner. This nine-foot-square room served as the apartment of Washington Irving when the Ameri-

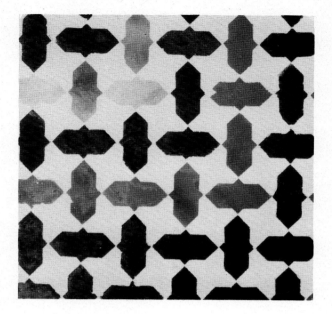

can author was writing *The Legends of the Alhambra,* sketches of the Moors and Spaniards. Charles's sojourn in the Alhambra unfortunately prompted him to design his Renaissance palace. Its construction (which was never entirely completed), besides disturbing the harmony of the Arab palace, also required the destruction of much of it, in particular the apartments used by guards and servants and the harem.

The eighteenth century initiated the Alhambra's most perilous season. Spain was ravaged by the contest between the Habsburgs and Bourbons for the Spanish throne. Philip V, the first Bourbon king, who came to the throne in 1700 and died in 1746, had even less sympathy for Islamic art than had Charles V. For his stay in the Alhambra he had the rooms redone in the Italian style, banishing much splendid decoration behind ugly partitions.

During the Peninsular War — its savagery immortalized by Goya — Napoleon's troops showed the Alhambra as scant respect as the seventeenth-century Turks had shown the Parthenon. Fate, believed in by the Arabs, or magic, luckily saved the Alhambra from effects similar to those caused by the explosion that had disembowelled Athena's temple. Even so, as the French under Count Sebastiani retreated, they blew up portions of the reddish walls and towers; an inscription on the walls of the Alhambra implies that only the heroism of a Spanish corporal prevented total devastation. A Spanish historian blames the French for destroying the Alhambra's Old Mosque. Built by Muhammad III in 1308, this had survived in a state of good preservation. A contemporary Arab account makes us sigh for its loss:

It is ornamented with Mosaic work, and exquisite tracery of the most beautiful and intricate patterns, intermixed with silver flowers and graceful arches, supported by innumerable pillars of polished marble; indeed, what with the solidity of the structure, which the Sultan inspected in person, the elegance of the design, and the beauty of the proportions, the building has not its like in this country; and I have frequently heard our best architects say that they had never seen or heard of a building which can be compared to it.

The next man to affect the Alhambra was the Duke of Wellington. The then Spanish king, Ferdinand VII, honored the duke — whom Englishmen were to honor by naming the California *Sequoia gigantea* the Wellingtonia — with a pheasant-stocked Spanish estate. In return the duke resolved to afforest the dry and eroded ascent to the Alhambra, an area that in Arab times was planted with roses, oranges, and myrtle. His shipment of English elms was to give the modern approach its pleasant but hardly Moorish air.

While the nineteenth century marked the end of any danger that the Alhambra might be deliberately destroyed by men, a damaging earthquake of 1821 emphasized its vulnerability to natural forces if men neglected it. The intellectual movements associated with the French Encyclopedists and such Romantic artists as Sir Walter Scott had begun to impose a new respect for history and its relics, even when these included non-Christian elements.

As early as the 1770's educated Spaniards had persuaded the Spanish government to commission the Royal Academy of Saint Ferdinand to instruct two

Tiles in a profusion of colors, types, designs, and combinations abound along the Alhambra walls, climb the columns, and decorate alcoves (right). Despite the dizzying richness of their variation, their ultimate effect is tranquillity. Most of the tiles in the Alhambra, as in other Nasrid buildings, were made in the ceramic workshops of Malaga, which were also renowned for glazed lusterware, as exemplified by the Alhambra Vase (see Contents page). Until it fell to the Catholic Sovereigns in 1487, the city and surroundings of Malaga were a part of the Nasrid kingdom of Granada.

architects and an officer of engineers to report upon the state of the Great Mosque in Cordoba and the Alhambra Palace. As a result, an illustrated volume on the *Antigüedades Arabes de España* was published in Madrid in 1780. This marked the beginning of an intellectual revolution that would culminate in making modern Madrid a leading center for Arabic studies. But initially those interested in investigating the Arab past had an uphill task. Pascual de Gayangos y Arce was only enabled to reopen the closed book of medieval Spain thanks to an Arabic history by al-Maqqari which covered the period from the conquest until 1492.

Yet, around 1840, when Gayangos y Arce was preparing his monumental work, he was refused access to the invaluable collection of Arabic manuscripts in the Escorial Library. "Strange to say, despite repeated applications, and the intervention of persons high in rank and influence, my request was positively denied, professedly on the plea that the Library could not be opened, a dispute having arisen between the Government and the Royal Household as to the possession of it." This obstruction was more likely the result of personal conflicts and bureaucracy than the earlier hostility of Catholic dynasts to Islamic relics. In 1830, the same king who later disputed the ownership of the Escorial manuscripts endowed the architect José Contreras with funds that enabled him to repair the Alhambra's fabric and to restore the tiles and arabesques. Since Philip V had been the last king to stay there, even those parts undamaged by war were in a sorry state. In this important charge Contreras was succeeded by his son and then his grandson. In 1870, the Alhambra was declared a national monument.

Thus miraculously the Alhambra has survived as chief symbol of the enduring if ambiguous link between the Arabs and Spain, a link that the assaults on the Islamic religion, the use of Arabic, and even such habits as bathing had not broken. Though the Islamic Allah yielded to the Holy Trinity, the exclamation *Ya 'Allah!* was too common to be expunged. It survived as *Olé!*

The thirteen towers of the Alhambra perimeter were given Spanish names. A tower on the southeast was consecrated to Saint John of the Cross, sixteenth-century Spain's greatest mystical poet. Yet many of the Christian poet's most typical terms for renunciation — purgation, emptiness, nakedness, liberation — had already been used by the fourteenth-century mystic ibn-Abbad, whose hometown, Ronda, was one of the last Andalusian cities to remain in Moorish hands. Even when the fall of Ronda (in 1485) was followed by that of Granada, the Moriscos of Andalusia kept alive the mystical tradition; Saint John of the Cross died twenty years before their expulsion. The religious passion that remained Spain's great positive force was in part a result of the Spaniards having so long shared their peninsula with the followers of Muhammad.

Language, as much as metaphysical outlook, is a transmittable and persistent part of a national culture. The Arabic influence on Spanish — as "Castilian" became — testifies to the depth of the interaction between the two peoples. Because of the skills of the Mudéjar craftsmen — the Muslims who stayed to work behind the advancing Christian lines and who built many churches for their new patrons — to this day, one expert writes, the technical Spanish words of the carpenter's trade are largely Arabic. Because the Arabs also excelled in all agricultural pursuits, the same expert tells us: . . . suburb, village, farm, are all known by Arabic words. The countryman measures his corn by the *fenega* of one and a half bushels (Ar. *faniqa,* a large sack), and divides it into twelve *celemines,* each equivalent to a gallon (Ar. *thamānī,* colloquial *zemenī,* eight), and he has another measure, the *arroba* (*al-rub'a*) a "quarter" (of a hundredweight) dry measure, or four gallons liquid. His entire vocabulary concerned with irrigation is Arabic, and so are the names of numerous flowers, fruits, vegetables, shrubs, and trees. Sugar (*azúcar*) has passed into Spanish, Portuguese, and other European languages through the Arabic *al-sukkar,* Persian *shakar,* and not (as is often stated in Spain) through the Latin *saccharum;* both words are derived ultimately, by different roads, from the same word in Sanskrit.

It takes a philologist to extricate the roots of Spanish nouns derived from Arabic. But many borrowings are easily identifiable to anyone who visits Spain. The Spaniards frequently incorporated the Arabic article *al* into the nouns they borrowed. Such words with included *al* are *arroz,* "rice" (Ar. *al-ruzz*); *alcoba,* "bedroom," (*al-qub-ba*); or *alcade,* "mayor," (*al-qādī,* judge). The place names of reconquered Spain have sometimes been baptized; more often they retain evidence of their Arabic past. Physical features such as mountain (Ar. *jabal*), cape (Ar. *taraf*), or island (Ar. *al-jazira*) survive, for example, in Monte Jabaluz, Trafalgar (*taraf al-ghār,* "cape of the cave"), and Algeciras. The most common of such features is the *wādī,* or river valley. Translated in Spanish as *guad,* it occurs in the "Large River" Guadalquivir (*Wādi al-Kabīr*), the

Anyplace else the palace built by Charles V (right) would be impressive, but its presence in the midst of the Alhambra makes it seem squat and heavy. It is said that a fire had destroyed a section of the Alhambra and the emperor then ordered further demolition to make room for his new edifice, razing servants' quarters and, most regrettably, the harem. Above are medallions showing Charles V (left) and his queen, Isabella of Portugal.

"River of Pomegranates" Guarroman (*Wādi al-Rumān*), or the "River of Cotton" Guadalcotón (*Wādi al-Qutn*). *Ramla,* a sandy riverbed, has given its name to the Ramblas, Barcelona's famous boulevard. Manmade institutions also survive in countless place names; the city (Ar. *medīna*) from Medina alone to Medina-Sidonia, Medina de Pomar, and others.

Many languages, including English, incorporate names taken straight from foreign tongues. But when a language borrows a common preposition or a grammatical structure, the link is evidently stronger. *Hasta mañana,* a phrase expressive of an easygoing way of life, goes back in more than spirit to the Alhambra. While *mañana* is Latin, the humble *hasta* is the Arabic *hattā,* meaning "until." (It is also borrowed in the Portuguese word *até.*)

Again, Andalus has given its impress to the major Spanish expression of the human ideal. *El hidalgo* can claim to be one of the most important ideals produced in the last three millennia. Its basic meaning, *hijo d'algo,* "son of something," originally denoted pecuniary worth, rather than virtue. But the term, which first became common for members of the lesser nobility, was coined, then worn smooth through handling by a society in which worth could be connected with genealogy, prowess, or poetry but owed nothing to money. And while *hijo* and *algo* derive from Latin, a leading Spanish lexicologist points out that it is typical of Arabic to employ *ibn,* "son" (the equivalent of *hijo*) with an abstraction; this construction invaded Spanish. For example, just as *ibn-al-sabil* ("son of the road") meant in Arabic "the traveler," *hijo di fortuna* meant "a lucky man." Thus in grammatical form as well as

Even in Spain the Arabs never forgot their desert origins, prizing water above all other elements. In addition to those gracing the Alhambra, the fountains of the Generalife give a dazzling display of nature's bounty and constitute a luxuriant oasis in the Andalusian hills.

interior content the word *hidalgo* shows that reconquered Andalus had conquered part of Castile as captured Athens had in turn captured part of Rome.

A characteristic of Andalus, even in its decline, had been its vigorous contacts, through pilgrims and travelers, with the world outside. A characteristic of its conquerors was their isolation. Spain became all but the Tibet of Europe. Ironically, the major factor in restoring the peninsula's connections with a larger world has been the ordinary man and woman, not the statesman or the intellectual. Since the early 1950's visitors in increasing multitudes have come to Spain, giving it the largest number of tourists of any country in Europe. The Alhambra has been high on most itineraries of Spain's visitors. This makes it difficult for today's traveler to recapture the peace in which Washington Irving studied the palace. The contemporary American writer Thomas E. Wright has vividly evoked a modern visitor's exasperation with his fellows:

Small Japanese men with cameras darted everywhere. Long-haired youths in Carnaby Street clothes failed to experience Beauty in the Court of the Myrtles due to a crowd there of Piccadilly Circus proportions. A flock of American tourists hurried through leaving behind a spoor of Kodak film wrappers. In dark corners mini-skirted *señoritas* kissed Dutch air-force pilots. A massive drove of communist tourists lumbered past, conducted by a brawny Russian woman with a downy upper lip. Guards coaxed an Australian down from an orange tree he had climbed for a photographic angle. A Mexican child vomited onto the Alhambra vase. An Irish youth pushed a Norwegian sailor in the Myrtles Pool. A Portuguese baby lost its

balance and fell from a parapet. "Sometimes," a custodian said, shaking his head, "I wish I were back in Madrid working in the brewery!"

Wright was maddened into resolving to spend a moonlit night alone inside the palace, which he contrived to do. When a ferocious watchdog made him surrender to the guard, the kindly captain allowed him to sleep in the Hall of the Two Sisters and in the morning take a solitary dip in the Pool of the Houris.

But for all their drawbacks, the tourists — you and I en masse — have restored to Andalus its sense of involvement with the outside world. By giving Spain a large balance of capital, they have helped turn a reactionary backwater into one of contemporary Europe's most dynamic economies.

The Alhambra has now spoken to more than seven centuries in the language of a beauty achieved from unlavish and sometimes rough materials. It was the product of a reduced and threatened state in a great tradition. This gives it importance to the twentieth century as a whole and to its builders in particular. For modern builders have a similar problem though it derives from a different cause. Population expansion rather than poverty compels the use of materials that can be cheaply mass produced, materials such as concrete, glass, and plastic. The Alhambra, austere without but ablaze within, shows the power of decoration to an age that has forgotten it.

To the world at large the Alhambra's intricate but tranquil arabesques, its disposal of water, sky, and plants, its massive Gate of Justice, hint that it may be possible to achieve, somewhere at some time, the harmonization of complexity without oppression.

THE ALHAMBRA
IN LITERATURE

A page decoration (opposite) taken
from a Mozarab manuscript of the
eleventh century shows the strong
influence Islam had on its Christian
progenitors. The illustrations on the
following pages give views and details
of the Alhambra and environs taken
from nineteenth-century sources.

The earliest records of fortifications on the hill now occupied by the Alhambra date from the mid-eighth century. But a picturesque episode that occurred in the ninth century furnishes the first literary mention of the al-Qal'ah al-Hamra *(the Red Citadel) at Granada. The 860's had witnessed civil wars up and down Andalus between pure-blooded Arabians and* Muladún, *or people of mixed blood. During one rainy autumn, the latter, commanded by Nabil, a Muslim of Christian extraction, besieged Granada's Arabian tribesmen who had taken refuge on the Alhambra hill. Among the besiegers was a bard, who composed the following verses and shot them over the walls, wrapped around an arrow.*

Deserted and roofless are the houses of our enemies; invaded by
    the fall rains, traversed by tempestuous winds.
Let them within the red citadel hold their mischievous councils;
    on every side perdition and woe surround them.

ANONYMOUS
860–65

THE NASRID CITADEL

The chronicler adds that the Arabian commander inside ordered his poet-in-residence to compose a suitable reply, but this did not survive. The construction of the present Alhambra Palace is ascribed to the Nasrid sultans of the first half of the fourteenth century. It is possible to form a clear picture of what Granada was like under the Nasrids, thanks to the monumental Comprehensive Book of Granada *(c. 1350) by the learned vizier Lisan-al-Din ibn-al-Khatib (1313–74). The author of more than sixty works on history, poetry, medicine, and mystico-philosophic subjects — much of which is extant — ibn-al-Khatib is remembered as one of Granada's greatest Muslim writers. The following account of his city and people comes from* The Shining Rays of the Full Moon: On the History of the Nasrid Dynasty, *which is ibn-al-Khatib's own condensed version of the* Comprehensive Book.*

In religious belief the people of Granada are orthodox and in no wise infected with subversive ideas, being adherents of Malakite doctrine. They are entirely obedient to the authorities and pay their taxes not only patiently but cheerfully. Physically pleasing as well, they are endowed with medium-sized noses, clear skin, and for the most part black hair. In stature, too, they are just right, neither too short nor too tall. They are well-spoken, and their Arabic is elegant although heavily spiced with localisms and marked with a certain tendency to longwindedness. In differences of opinion they are proud and obstinate. A great number of them are Berbers and foreigners (Spaniards).

In winter, the majority wear clothes of colors corresponding to their fortune and quality; but in summertime they affect garments of the most expensive striped Persian linen, silk, cotton, or mohair, African jellabas, and Tunisian chiffon so fine that veils made of it must be worn doubled. Thus you may behold them in the mosques, like flowers of the field on a pleasant springtime day.

Their regular army consists of two types of troops, Andalusian and Berber. The Andalusians are commanded by a chief who is a relative of the Sultan or one of his favorites. Their arms and armor were formerly like those of their Spanish neighbors, wearing bulky corselets, slung-on shields, heavy bronze helmets, and carrying broad-headed lances. Thus accoutered, and

mounted in awkward saddles with great lubberly hindbows, the noble Grana-dines of old sallied forth, followed by standard-bearers, and each of them could be recognized by the distinctive mark and insignia peculiar to his arms. With the passage of time, however, these things have fallen into disuse, and the present generation wear short corselets and lightweight gilded helmets, using Arabian saddles, shields of antelope hide, and short spears.

As for the Berber troops, they are of several different nationalities — Marinid, Ziyanid, Tiganid, and Ajisid tribesmen, Arabians and North Afri-cans — having their own commanders who are in turn subordinate to a commander-in-chief having authority over all ranks of officers. The com-mander-in-chief always belongs to a distinguished Marinid tribe and is thus related to the Sultan of Western Africa. Standard headgear for these troops is the turban (worn but little otherwise in Granada except by religious teachers and judges and members of the learned professions). Their favorite weapons are the crossbow and a sort of dart-tipped javelin with a throwstrap at mid-shaft which is grasped at the moment of hurling. They train daily, and target practice is a required part of their training.

The buildings of Granada are of no more than average size and value. Their festivals and other holiday events are splendid to the eye but not ruin-ous to the purse. Because the youth of Granada are unusually musical, public houses with music are extremely popular.

Bread is in plenty, for the most part of high-quality wheat, although the poor and laboring classes (in winter especially) live on an excellent barley-bread, which is in fact more nourishing than any other kind of cereal food. Fruit is abundant in Granada, the grape in particular. At the present time, some fourteen thousand vineyards great and small are listed in the annual tax-rolls of the kingdom. In addition, there are large quantities of dried fruits throughout the year. Grapes are stored nine months out of twelve without spoilage; the people also lay in great stocks of figs, raisins, apples, pomegranates, chestnuts, acorns, almonds, and other nuts, which are thus in short supply at times of the year when they are not eaten anyway.

Their coinage is of fine silver and gold bullion alloyed with pure additives in exact proportions. No coin on earth is superior to theirs.

Each year during the harvest season it is their custom to move with wives and children and everything they own out of the city and onto their country properties, where they camp out, relying on their own superior courage and arms to protect themselves from the nearby foe, whose land lies within view of theirs.

Their commonest personal adornments are of silver: silver necklaces, bangles, bracelets, and ankle-rings. However, precious stones such as sap-phires, topaz, emeralds, and the choicest pearls are also frequently met with in families associated with the royal house or with a tribe of old and dis-tinguished name. The ladies of Granada are in fact lovely, being moderately plump with firm, voluptuous curves and long, sleek hair. Their mouths smell good, and they are given to wearing fresh-scented perfumes. They are lively, move with grace, and speak with elegance, charm, and wit. Tall women are however a rarity. In our day they have reached the extreme limits of what can be achieved in the arts of toilette and coiffure, harmonizing these with different-colored layers of fabric, vying with one another in lavish displays of embroidered cloth-of-gold and brocade and other alluring finery, and (in a word) carrying luxury to the point of lunacy. . . .

139

Now of the Sultans of Granada who are styled Nasrids, the first and foremost was Muhammad ibn-Yusuf ibn-Nasr (Ibn al-Ahmar) . . . . Born of noble parents, he was reared in the study and admiration of great men. When still a youth the blood boiled in his veins and he was consumed with a desire for power, and thus embarked on mighty undertakings. . . .

Soon after he became ruler of Granada, he decided to build a fortress on the Alhambra Hill. Lacking the necessary funds, he imposed certain taxes upon his subjects for the construction of the said building, at which he was not only present but in charge. And when the work was complete, he provided it with an abundant water supply and made his palace there. Allied at first with neighboring kings, he began to prosper so much that he heaped the royal treasury with gold and silver and filled the granaries and storehouses adjacent to the Alhambra with grain, peas, beans, clover, alfalfa, and other kinds of food and fodder in great plenty. And he fortified the Alhambra Hill with guardtowers, an arsenal, and an unbroken defensive enceinte, and thus very happily kept what his ingenuity of thought and deed had won.

> IBN-AL-KHATIB
> *The Shining Rays of the Full Moon:*
> *On the History of the Nasrid Dynasty, c.* 1360

The Arabic inscriptions, which are everywhere intertwined with the ornamentation of the Alhambra, furnish striking evidence of how completely the Spanish Muslims' religious beliefs and modes of thought were bound up with their art and architecture. The inscriptions are of three kinds: verses from the Koran, traditional religious sayings, and poems praising the builders and owners of the Alhambra. The poems are attributed to the statesman Abu Abd Allah ibn-Zamrak (1333–93?) who was the protégé of the already-quoted historian and vizier ibn-al-Khatib. The Koranic and traditional sentences toward the end of this selection are as omnipresent as the God they praise.

At the entrance to the Court of the Myrtles:

The best praise be given to God. I will remove all the effects of a malicious eye upon our master Yusuf by repeating these five sentences, which are like so many verses from the Koran: "I flee for refuge to the master of the creatures." "Praise to God the only one." "Thanks to God." "He is eternal." "His is the power."

By the sun and its rising brightness, by the moon when she follows him, by the day when he shows its splendor, by the night when it covers him with darkness, by the heaven and Him who built it, by the earth and Him who spread it forth, by the soul and by Him who completely formed it, and inspired into it wickedness and piety, there is no god but God!

Court of the Myrtles:

Blessed be He who entrusted to you the command of His servants through you, to extend and benefit Islam!

For how many cities of the infidels came you to in the morning, whose inhabitants saw you in the evening the sole arbiter of their lives!

When you put on their necks the yoke of the captives, that they might appear in the ensuing morning building your palaces in servitude.

You conquered Andalus by force of arms, thereby opening to victory a gate that was shut before.

And prior to that exploit you subdued twenty fortresses, making all things within a prey to your warriors.

Indeed if Islam could choose what it most desires, it would certainly choose that you live and be safe forever.

Since the fires of excellence shine at your door, generosity itself smiles. while regarding them with an approving eye.

Excellence whose traces are visible in your every action, more transparent and bright than pearls when threaded.

O, son of eminence, prudence, wisdom, courage and liberality! in whom these virtues out-top the stars in the sky.

You have risen in the horizon of empire like the sun in the vault of heaven, mercifully to dissipate the intervening shadows of injustice and oppression.

You have secured even the tender branches from the breath of the summer gale, and frightened the very stars in the vault of heaven.

For if the planets quiver in their orbits, it is only through dread of you; and if the boughs of the eastern willow bow down, it is to be thanking you forever.

At the entrance from the Court of the Myrtles to the Hall of the Blessing:

1.

I am like the nuptial array of a bride, endowed with every beauty and perfection. . . .

Look at this vase, and you will easily understand all the truth of my assertion.

Examine also my tiara, you will find it resembles the bright halo of the full moon.

For truly ibn-Nasr is the sun of this orb shining in splendor and beauty.

May he continue in the noontide zenith of his glory, secure from all attacks, when the time for declension is arrived.

2.

I am an honor to blessing; I am a sign by which felicity itself is enhanced.

You may imagine the vase within to be like a devout man always standing to perform his prayers.

Who no sooner has said one, than he hastens again to repeat it.

Truly, through my Lord ibn-Nasr, God has ennobled his servants. . . .

Hall of the Ambassadors:

From me you are welcomed morning and evening by the tongues of blessing, prosperity, happiness, and friendship.

That is the elevated dome, and we (the several recesses) are her daughters; yet I possess excellence and dignity above all those of my race.

Surely we are all parts of the same body; but I am like the heart in the midst of the rest; and from the heart springs all energy of soul and life.

True, my fellows here may be compared to the signs of the Zodiac in the heaven of that dome: but I can boast what they are lacking, the honor of a Sun —

Since my lord, the victorious Yusuf, has decorated me with the robes of his glory and excellence without disguise,

And has made me the throne of his empire: may its eminence be upheld by the Master of Divine Glory and the Celestial Throne!

Hall of the Two Sisters:

1.

I am the garden, and every morn I am revealed in new beauty. Observe my dress attentively, and you will reap the benefit of a commentary on decoration.

For, by God! the elegant buildings by which I am surrounded certainly surpass all other buildings in the happy presage attending their foundation.

How many delightful prospects I enfold! How many objects, in the contemplation of which a highly gifted mind finds the gratification of its utmost wishes! . . .

For how many are the gorgeous robes in which you, O Sultan, have attired it, which surpass, in brilliancy of color, the vaunted robes of Yemen!

To look at them, one would imagine them to be so many planets revolving on the arches of this court as on their orbits, in order to throw in the shade even the first rays of morning.

Here are columns ornamented to absolute perfection, and the beauty of which has become proverbial; columns

Which, when struck by the rays of the rising sun, one might imagine, notwithstanding their colossal dimensions, to be so many blocks of pearl.

Indeed, we never saw a palace more lofty than this in its exterior, or more brilliantly decorated in its interior; or having more extensive apartments —

Markets they are, where those provided with money are paid in beauty, and where the judge of elegance is perpetually sitting to pronounce sentence.

Which, when the breath of the zephyr expires before the noontide rays, appear surrounded by a light which throws into shade all other light.

Victory and I are twin sisters; we are equally striking, we are identical in splendor.

2.

Brightly as the full moon does our Sultan shine in the high regions of the empire. May his praiseworthy deeds last forever, and his radiance never tarnish!

For what else is he but the sun? . . .

From me as from the horizon to overlook the court of his empire, whenever he appears on the throne of the Caliphs, like a bright luminary in the sky.

Let him but direct a glance to the quarter where the zephyrs joyfully play, and the fugitive gales shall instantly return to their usual abode.

Apartments are there enfolding so many wonders that the eyes of the spectator remain forever fixed upon them, provided he be gifted with a mind to appreciate them.

Wherein the warm gale descends to mitigate the cold of winter, thereby producing a salubrious air and a mild temperature.

Truly so many are the beauties of every kind that we enfold, that even the

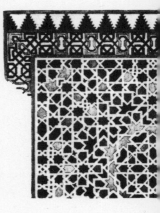

stars in heaven come down to borrow their light from us.

And how can it be otherwise, when we are built by the command of a King whose illustrious deeds and commendable actions are already recorded by the historians?

3.

Praise to God!

With my ornaments and tiara I surpass beauty itself: nay, the luminaries in the Zodiac out of envy descend to me.

The water-vase within me, they say, is like a devout man . . . ready to begin his prayers.

Against the current of time my generous deeds are ensured. I shall always quench the thirst of the thirsty, and remedy the wants of the needy.

Indeed, it looks as if I had borrowed generosity itself from the hands of our Lord Abu-l-Hajaj.

May he continue to shine a great luminary in the sky, as long as the full moon beams forth through the shadows of night.

4.

Praise to God!

Delicately have the fingers of the artist embroidered my robe, after setting the jewels of my diadem.

People compare me to the throne of a bride, yet I surpass it in this: I can guarantee the happiness of those who possess me.

If anyone approach me complaining of thirst, he will . . . receive cool and limpid water, sweet without admixture.

As if I were the bow of the clouds where it first appears, and the sun of our Lord Abu-l-Hajaj.

A monarch whose hands distribute gifts to the needy as often and profusely as the waves of the sea succeed each other.

May his court be revered and visited as long as the house of God in Mecca shall continue the resort of pilgrims.

5.

Every art has gifted me with its elegance — nay, has given me all its splendor and perfection.

Those who behold me take me for a female addressing this vase, whose favors as her beloved she wishes to obtain.

Indeed, when the spectator has attentively examined my beauty, he will find reality to exceed the most extravagant conception of his fancy.

He will see the full moon beam forth from the rays of my light, and its halo leave me to enter the mansions of the sky.

This is a palace of transparent crystal; those who look at it imagine it to be a boundless ocean.

And yet I am not alone to be wondered at, for I overlook in astonishment a garden, the like of which no human eyes ever saw.

I was built by the Imam ibn-Nasr. May God uphold his majesty as a pattern to other kings!

And perpetuate his high station and glorious rank as long as (like the sun or the full moon) he continues to rise in the high regions of the sky.

Court of the Lions (inscription around the basin of the fountain):

Blessed be He who gave the Imam Muhammad a mansion which in beauty exceeds all other mansions . . .

Here is the garden containing wonders of art the like of which God forbids should elsewhere be found.

Look at this solid mass of pearl, glistening all around and spreading through the air its showers of prismatic bubbles.

While it falls within a circle of silvery froth, and then flows amid other jewels surpassing everything in beauty, even exceeding the marble itself in whiteness and transparency.

To look at the basin, one would imagine it to be a mass of solid ice, and the water to melt from it; yet, it is impossible to say which of the two is really flowing.

Don't you see how the water from above flows on the surface, notwithstanding how the current underneath strives to oppose its progress?

Like a lover whose eyes are brimming with tears, yet he suppresses them for fear of a talebearer.

For truly: what else is this fountain but a beneficent cloud pouring out its abundant supplies over the lions underneath?

Like the hands of the Caliph when he rises in the morning to distribute plentiful rewards among his soldiers the lions of war . . .

And O heir of the Nasrids! To you belongs that ancestral pride which makes you look with contempt on the kings of all other countries.

May the blessings of God forever be with you! May He make your subjects obedient to your rule, and grant you victory over all your enemies!

In all parts of the palace, interwoven with ornaments:

Praise be given to God the only one.
Praise be given to God. There is no power or strength
but in God.
There is no god but God; Muhammad is His messenger.
Immutability is God's.
O God! Yours is the praise forever; and yours are
the thanks forever.
Praise be given to God, for His bestowing on us
the blessings of Islam.
There is no conqueror but God.
God is the best of protectors, He is the most
compassionate of the compassionate.
God always was true in His words.
God is our refuge in every trouble.
And there is no help to be had except from God,
the illustrious, the omnipotent.
Whatever you possess of the good things of this world
comes from God.
The blessing comes from God.
Glory to our Lord, the Sultan Abu-l-Hajaj.
Glory to our Lord, the Sultan Abu-Abdullah.
Glory to our Lord, the Sultan Abu-Abdullah

Al-ghani-billah ("the rich in God").
Glory to our Lord, the warlike and just Sultan
Abu-Abdullah Al-ghani-billah.

May divine help, solidity of empire, and splendid victory over the enemy fall to the lot of our Lord Abu-l-Hajaj, commander of the Muslims!

May power everlasting and imperishable glory be the lot of the owner of this palace.

Verses from the KORAN *and poems attributed to* IBN-ZAMRAK
Inscribed inside the Alhambra, c. 1350

DEEDS OF DARKNESS

All three of the great men responsible for the completion and final perfection of the Alhambra died violent deaths. Sultan Yusuf died in 1354, in the Alhambra itself, at the hands of a crazed assassin. Some twenty years later, chief minister and historian ibn-al-Khatib was accused of heresy and ignominiously strangled in a Moroccan jail cell, after a mock trial presided over by his student and successor as chief minister, ibn-Zamrak. The latter continued another fifteen years in his duties as chief minister and court poet when sometime in about 1393 he was murdered together with his sons on the new sultan's orders. These events are recounted in the monumental History of the Mohammedan Dynasties of Spain *by the Algerian historian Ahmed al-Maqqari (c. 1591–1632). This selection from al-Maqqari's* History *opens with the assassination of Sultan Yusuf.*

Yusuf Abu al-Hejaj was one of the most enlightened sovereigns of the Nasrid dynasty. In his days justice was administered with an even hand, literature and science flourished, and public order prevailed. Unluckily for the Muslims of Andalus, his reign did not last long; for, in the year 755 (beginning Jan. 25, A.D. 1354), he was assassinated by a madman whilst performing his devotions in the mosque of his palace. The event is thus described in a letter which the Vizir Ibn al-Khatib addressed . . . to Abu 'Inan Faris, Sultan of Western Africa.

As Yusuf Abu al-Hejaj was performing the last prostration of his prayer, a madman rushed upon him and wounded him with a *khanjar* or yataghan. The assassin was immediately seized. The Sultan, who had been mortally wounded, made some signs, as if he wished to speak; but, after uttering a few unintelligible words, he was carried senseless to his palace, where he died shortly after his arrival. The assassin, in the meantime, was given up to the infuriated mob, who lynched him and burned his body. Abu al-Hejaj was interred on the evening of Sunday within the Alhambra, in the cemetery reserved for the princes of the royal family. He left three sons: Muhammad, who succeeded him; Isma'il, and Qays.

Muhammad, surnamed *Al-ghani-billah* (he who is rich in God), succeeded. Some time after his accession he dispatched to Fez his Vizir, Lisan al-Din Ibn al-Khatib, with instructions to implore the aid of Sultan Abu 'Inan Faris against the common foe. Upon being introduced to the Sultan's presence, and before he had delivered the message of which he was the bearer, Ibn al-Khatib uttered extempore some verses which called forth the admiration of all present, and were so much approved of by the Sultan that before listening to what Ibn al-Khatib had to say, he told him, "By God! I do not know what the object of your visit is, but whatever it may be, I from this moment grant your request." And so he did — for, after loading him with presents of all kinds, he promised to send troops to the assistance of his master, and dismissed him highly pleased and satisfied with the result of his mission. The circumstance elicited from the celebrated Qadi Abu al-Qasim al-Sharif, who formed also part of the embassy, the very just remark, that there never was an ambassador who obtained the object of his mission before he had made it known, except Ibn al-Khatib.

"Muhammad had reigned scarcely five years," says the historian Ibn Khaldun, "when a half-brother of his, named Isma'il, assisted by another of his relatives, of the name of Abu Sa'id, revolted in Granada; and, taking advantage of the absence of the Sultan, who was then residing at a country place outside of the Alhambra, scaled at night the walls of that fortress, and made himself master of it, after putting to death Redwan, the Vizir of Muhammad. This took place on the 27th day of Ramadan, 760 (Aug. 23, A.D. 1359), and, on the following day, Isma'il Abu al-Walid was proclaimed by the troops and the citizens.

"In the meantime the dethroned Sultan, having found means to escape from his pursuers, repaired to Guadix, where he established his authority. When the news of this revolution and the murder of Redwan reached Fez, the Sultan, Abu Salim, was highly displeased, for he was the friend both of Muhammad and his minister. He sent immediately to Andalus a theologian of his court, named Abu al-Qasim Ibn Sharif with instructions to invite the deposed Sultan to his court. On his arrival at Granada, Abu al-Qasim negotiated with the great officers of the state and the ministers of the usurper, that Muhammad should be allowed to leave Guadix and proceed to Africa unmolested, and that all those individuals who had been arrested and imprisoned for their fidelity to the deposed Sultan should be set at liberty. In their number was Ibn al-Khatib, who, owing to his intimacy with the Vizir Redwan, and his well-known attachment to the dethroned Sultan, had been confined to prison. Another writer says that Ibn al-Khatib owed his liberation to Ibn Marzuk, the Vizir of Abu Salim, who was an old friend of his ever since his stay in Granada; for he had no sooner heard of his friend's imprisonment than he prevailed upon his master the Sultan, whose confidence he enjoyed, to send an embassy to Andalus. However this may be, Ibn al-Khatib was released and allowed to proceed to Guadix in company with Abu al-Qasim, the African ambassador. On his arrival there, Ibn al-Khatib found his master preparing to cross over to Africa. Muhammad took his departure and accompanied him and arrived in this country at the end of 760 (Nov., A.D. 1359). On the news of Muhammad's approach, Abu Salim went out in state to receive him, and he was soon after admitted into a hall of the royal palace crowded with courtiers, theologians, poets, and doctors. It was on this occasion that his Vizir, Ibn al-Khatib, uttered extempore that celebrated ode of his, rhyming in *ra*, the argument of which was to implore his aid in favor of his master, and to ask him to restore him to the possession of his throne.

"O Vicar of God! May the Almighty increase your power as the full moon shines through the shadow of night.

"May the hands of His omnipotence avert from you that evil against which mortals have no power."

Ibn Khaldun, from whom the above details are borrowed, says, "Such was the effect produced upon the audience by Ibn al-Khatib's verses that they were unable to suppress their tears. When the interview was over, Muhammad retired to the palace which had been prepared for him, the apartments of which he found strewn with the finest carpets, and the stables well provided with generous steeds, their trappings and saddles ornamented with gold. Handsome robes of the most costly stuffs were sent in, as well as slave girls for him and those of his suite; in short, nothing was wanting to make their residence at court agreeable. Muhammad, moreover, was treated with every distinction, and, whether he rode or walked out of his palace, the same honors were paid to him as to the Sultan, only that Muhammad would never assume the titles of royalty, out of respect for his host. Muhammad and his suite stayed at Fez until the year 763, when they all returned to Andalus, and that Sultan regained possession of his throne."

AHMED AL-MAQQARI
History of the Mohammedan Dynasties of Spain, c. 1620

The capture of Granada by Ferdinand and Isabella in 1492 has perhaps never been more spiritedly told than by the anonymous author of the following ballad, "The Flight from Granada," which was composed within the first two or three generations following the event.

There was crying in Granada when the sun was going down;
Some calling on the Trinity — some calling on Mahoun.
Here passed away the Koran — there in the Cross was borne —
And here was heard the Christian bell — and there the Moorish horn;

Te Deum Laudamus! was up the Alcala sung:
Down from the Alhambra's minarets were all the crescents flung;
The arms thereon of Arragon they with Castile's display;
One King comes in in triumph — one weeping goes away.

Thus cried the weeper, while his hands his old white beard did tear,
"Farewell, farewell, Granada! thou city without peer!
Woe, woe, thou pride of Heathendom! seven hundred years and more
Have gone since first the Faithful thy royal sceptre bore!

"Thou wert the happy mother of an high renowned race;
Within thee dwelt a haughty line that now go from their place;
Within thee fearless knights did dwell, who fought with mickle glee —
The enemies of proud Castile — the bane of Christentie!

"The mother of fair dames wert thou, of truth and beauty rare,
Into whose arms did courteous knights for solace sweet repair;
For whose dear sakes the gallants of Afric made display
Of might in joust and battle on many a bloody day.

"Here, gallants held it little thing for ladies' sake to die,
Or for the Prophet's honour, and pride of Soldanry;
For here did valour flourish, and deeds of warlike might
Ennobled lordly palaces in which was our delight.

"The gardens of thy Vega, its fields and blooming bowers —
Woe, woe! I see their beauty gone and scattered all their flowers!
No reverence can he claim — the King that such a land hath lost —
On charger never can he ride, nor be heard among the host;
But in some dark and dismal place, where none his face may see,
There, weeping and lamenting, alone that King should be." —

Thus spake Granada's King as he was riding to the sea,
About to cross Gibraltar's Strait away to Barbary:
Thus he in heaviness of soul unto his Queen did cry —
(He had stopped and ta'en her in his arms, for together they did fly).

"Unhappy King! whose craven soul can brook" (she 'gan reply)
"To leave behind Granada — who has not heart to die! —
Now for the love I bore thy youth, thee gladly could I slay
For what is life to leave when such a crown is cast away?"

ANONYMOUS
Translated by JOHN GIBSON LOCKHART
"The Flight from Granada," c. 1500

THE LAST SIGH OF THE MOOR

The locus classicus for the fall of Granada remains the narrative of it given by William Hickling Prescott (1796–1859) in his three-volume History of the Reign of Ferdinand and Isabella the Catholic, *which sold out within a month of its appearance on Christmas Day, 1838 and made him famous. The present account of the events of January 2, 1492, in Granada was put together by Prescott after a painstaking comparison of state papers relating to the taking of the city and of numerous eyewitness accounts, both published and unpublished, on the Spanish side. According to more recently published Arabic sources which were not available to Prescott but which were also based on eyewitness accounts on the Islamic side, Ferdinand did not treat Abdallah (Boabdil) with "sympathy and regard" (as Prescott says) but with undisguised rudeness and contempt.*

Every preparation was made by the Spaniards for performing this last act of the drama with suitable pomp and effect. The mourning which the court had put on for the death of Prince Alonso of Portugal, occasioned by a fall from his horse a few months after his marriage with the infanta Isabella, was exchanged for gay and magnificent apparel. On the morning of the 2d, the whole Christian camp exhibited a scene of the most animating bustle. The grand cardinal Mendoza was sent forward at the head of a large detachment, comprehending his household troops, and the veteran infantry grown grey in the Moorish wars, to occupy the Alhambra preparatory to the entrance of the sovereigns. Ferdinand stationed himself at some distance in the rear, near an Arabian mosque, since consecrated as the hermitage of St. Sebastion. He was surrounded by his courtiers, with their stately retinues, glittering in gorgeous panoply, and proudly displaying the armorial bearings of their ancient houses. The queen halted still farther in the rear, at the village of Armilla.

As the column under the grand cardinal advanced up the Hill of Martyrs, over which a road had been constructed for the passage of the artillery, he was met by the Moorish prince Abdallah, attended by fifty cavaliers, who descending the hill rode up to the position occupied by Ferdinand on the banks

of the Xenil. As the Moor approached the Spanish king, he would have thrown himself from his horse, and saluted his hand in token of homage, but Ferdinand hastily prevented him, embracing him with every mark of sympathy and regard. Abdallah then delivered up the keys of the Alhambra to his conqueror saying, "They are thine, O king, since Allah so decrees it; use thy success with clemency and moderation." Ferdinand would have uttered some words of consolation to the unfortunate prince, but he moved forward with dejected air to the spot occupied by Isabella, and, after similar acts of obeisance, passed on to join his family, who had preceded him with his most valuable effects on the route to the Alpuxarras.

The sovereigns during this time waited with impatience the signal of the occupation of the city by the cardinal's troops, which, winding slowly along the outer circuit of the walls, as previously arranged, in order to spare the feelings of the citizens as far as possible, entered by what is now called the gate of Los Molinos. In a short time, the large silver cross, borne by Ferdinand throughout the crusade, was seen sparkling in the sun-beams, while the standards of Castile and St. Jago waved triumphantly from the red towers of the Alhambra. At this glorious spectacle, the choir of the royal chapel broke into the solemn anthem of the Te Deum, and the whole army, penetrated with deep emotion, prostrated themselves on their knees in adoration of the Lord of hosts, who had at length granted the consummation of their wishes, in this last and glorious triumph of the Cross. The grandees who surrounded Ferdinand then advanced towards the queen, and kneeling down saluted her hand in token of homage to her as sovereign of Granada. The procession took up its march towards the city, "the king and queen moving in the midst," says an historian, "emblazoned with royal magnificence; and, as they were in the prime of life, and had now achieved the completion of this glorious conquest, they seemed to represent even more than their wonted majesty. Equal with each other, they were raised far above the rest of the world. They appeared, indeed, more than mortal, and as if sent by Heaven for the salvation of Spain."

In the mean while the Moorish king, traversing the route of the Alpuxarras, reached a rocky eminence which commanded a last view of Granada. He checked his horse, and, as his eye for the last time wandered over the scenes of his departed greatness, his heart swelled, and he burst into tears. "You do well," said his more masculine mother, "to weep like a woman, for what you could not defend like a man!" "Alas!" exclaimed the unhappy exile, "when were woes ever equal to mine!" The scene of this event is still pointed out to the traveller by the people of the district; and the rocky height, from which the Moorish chief took his sad farewell of the princely abodes of his youth, is commemorated by the poetical title of *El Ultimo Sospiro del Moro,* "The Last Sigh of the Moor."

The sequel of Abdallah's history is soon told. Like his uncle, El Zagal, he pined away in his barren domain of the Alpuxarras, under the shadow, as it were, of his ancient palaces. In the following year, he passed over to Fez with his family, having commuted his petty sovereignty for a considerable sum of money paid him by Ferdinand and Isabella, and soon after fell in battle in the service of an African prince, his kinsman. "Wretched man," exclaims a caustic chronicler of his nation, "who could lose his life in another's cause, though he did not dare to die in his own. Such," continues the Arabian, with characteristic resignation, "was the immutable decree of destiny. Blessed be Allah, who exalteth and debaseth the kings of the earth, according to his divine will, in whose fulfilment consists that eternal justice, which regulates all human affairs." The portal, through which King Abdallah for the last time issued from his capital, was at his request walled up, that none other might again pass through it. In this condition it remains to this day, a memorial of the sad destiny of the last of the kings of Granada.

The fall of Granada excited general sensation throughout Christendom, where it was received as counterbalancing, in a manner, the loss of Constantinople, nearly half a century before. At Rome, the event was commemorated by a solemn procession of the pope and cardinals to St. Peter's, where high mass was celebrated, and the public rejoicing continued for several days. The intelligence was welcomed with no less satisfaction in England, where Henry the Seventh was seated on the throne.

WILLIAM HICKLING PRESCOTT
*History of the Reign of
Ferdinand and Isabella the Catholic,* 1838

WESTERN VISITORS

During the generation following 1492 the Alhambra was much used by Ferdinand and Isabella, and with the accession of Holy Roman Emperor Charles V to the Spanish throne in 1516, the Alhambra became a favorite imperial residence. In 1526, the Alhambra was the scene of a state visit by Count Palatine Frederick II. With him was his personal physician, Dr. Johannes Lange, who at forty was already known as one of the leading medical men of the day. His Epistolae medicinales *(1554), long a standard text, spoke of the construction of "the baths of the kings of Mauretania in the Alhambra fortress at Hispanic Granada" as a model of the ideal therapeutic bathing establishment. Though an admirer of the Alhambra, Dr. Lange was an enemy of Islam; his diary vividly records the tension between Granada's Christian and Muslim communities after the reconquest.*

The capital of the Kingdom of Granada is a city of the same name which surmounts the hills upon which it is built in such a way that no high spot or position outside its walls may command the whole place. Granada is almost twice the size of Nuremberg, and in the neighboring mountains, even on the hottest days of the year, there is a mighty abundance of snow, which they use to chill their wine. This town of Granada lies scarce a dozen leagues from the Mediterranean Sea. One may thus be in Africa within the space of three days, and in four days one may come to the extreme western limit of the world.

In former times Granada belonged to the white Moors, had two kings during its latter-day wars, and was besieged six years by King Ferdinand, whose army built a small city, Santa Fe, at its gates and whose queen, Isabella, captured it in the seventh year for our Holy Faith.

Also: half the population are white Moors, whose women and girls all wear white sailors' pants and pantaloons (almost like sheep-herders in Germany), and the said women also envelop themselves in white wraps that cover them from their face to their calves — but above all, they cover their faces. And in order that this custom of dress be freely permitted them, each must pay the Emperor an annual tax of one ducat; and such as stay away from church on Sundays must pay the priest one *real* each year. And on the hillsides of this city there are still deep caves to be seen in which Christian prisoners (among them a Bishop) were locked up at night and rented out by day to be exploited for manual labor of any kind.

Also: the aforesaid city was taken on Saint John's Day, and for this reason, every year on that day the nobles and burghers dress up like Moriscos and Turks with shields and lances and hold a mummery procession through the town at dawn. Later in the day they hold a mock triumph. Then they let loose six or seven bulls in the marketplace for the common folk to run with, and bait. Then comes the cavalry, rigged out like Turks and Moors and divided into two troops. Blazing away at each other with fat old hackbutts loaded with blank charges, they chase to and fro in mock fright, pursuing and retreating, making gallant stands.

We saw the Emperor himself play at this game at Granada, in the presence of her Imperial Majesty and a crowd of Portuguese ladies-in-waiting, on the Feast of Saint John the Baptist. And on that same day three men were mortally wounded by the bulls, and an old horse was accidentally shot in the head and laid out on the spot.

Also: the aforesaid Moors are forbidden (on the pain of heavy penalties) to bear arms, whether in the countryside or in their houses, apart from a short breadknife and a carving knife for cutting up meat (they eat no game, but all their meat comes from caged or chained or fenced-in creatures). And to this purpose the magistrates cause their houses to be searched twice a month.

Also: on our last day at Granada, the Emperor invited my lord to preside with him at a Moorish spectacle in a garden at the foot of Alhambra Hill. Adorned with remarkably fine pearls and precious stones all about their necks, ears, and arms, and dressed (almost like deacons at Mass) according to the custom of their land, they danced to the sound of lutes, fiddles, and drums, after which three fifty-year-old women and one who was about forty played and sang at the same time in unseemly heathenish strains, while the others clapped their hands in rhythm and shouted for joy.

After the dance, some Moorish women went up on the hillside and danced on a tightrope stretched between two chestnut trees, and then boldly spread their legs and made faces at the Emperor, screeching in their native tongue:

"Any that liveth here can get to Heaven!"

After this performance they were given a drink of water.

Also: the Moorish girls of Castile stain their fingernails bright orange, using henna. This (they fancy) makes them especially attractive. In my opinion, it makes them just like our good-for-nothing tanners at Nuremberg. They also think it a great reproach, if a young woman takes even a sip of wine. Therefore they all drink water.

In the aforesaid city of Granada they make all sorts of garments of silk, but all of it black, having no fast dyes of other colors, and it is scarcely if at all cheaper than in German lands, with the notable exception of double taffeta, which is very fine here. And pearls there are also cheap.

There are splendid vineyards and a great winepress next to the city walls. Also, there was at first no room for my lord's retinue in the palace, and for two days we slept on the ground and then rented bedrolls from the white Moors, who also required a deposit of fifteen ducats.

We were a fortnight at Granada, and on the seventh day of July by God's grace we went on our way rejoicing.

Also: the Emperor's palace was built by Moriscos on the Alhambra Hill within the city walls, and therein you may still see the curious and splendid baths of the Moorish king, who bathed there with his wives, of which he had as many as he pleased, and the one he desired to see after the bath he sent an apple to.

The water that flows through the aforesaid palace (in which there is also a fishpond) flows through almost every other noteworthy house in town. The water is insalubrious, and one may easily come down with dysentery from it; but they have no other water there, nor any wells, either.

DR. JOHANNES LANGE
Diary, 1526

By the time Washington Irving's Tales of the Alhambra *(1829) had been translated and published all over Europe and everywhere greeted as a masterpiece, the Romantic Alhambra craze was already in full spate. Chateaubriand, the famous author of* Atala *and* René, *had only recently created a tremendous stir with his* Last of the Abencerrages, *a marvelously silly love story set in the Alhambra, and in 1828 Victor Hugo's popular* Orientales *took up the war cry with a vengeance: "Granada has the Alhambra! Alhambra! Alhambra!" But Irving's book overshadowed all else, and there can be no doubt that the rescue of the Alhambra from complete disintegration was largely due to it. Irving lived in Spain from 1826 to 1829, and again from 1842 to 1846, as United States minister. The following account dates from the spring of 1828.*

To the traveller imbued with a feeling for the historical and poetical, so inseparably intertwined in the annals of romantic Spain, the Alhambra is as much an object of devotion as is the Caaba to all true Moslems. How many legends and traditions, true and fabulous, — how many songs and ballads, Arabian and Spanish, of love and war and chivalry, are associated with this Oriental pile! It was the royal abode of the Moorish kings, where, surrounded with the splendors and refinements of Asiatic luxury, they held dominion over what they vaunted as a terrestrial paradise, and made their last stand for empire in Spain. The royal palace forms but a part of a fortress, the walls of which, studded with towers, stretch irregularly round the whole crest of a hill, a spur of the Sierra Nevada or Snowy Mountains, and overlook the city; externally it is a rude congregation of towers and battlements, with no regularity of plan nor grace of architecture, and giving little promise of the grace and beauty which prevail within.

In the time of the Moors the fortress was capable of containing within its outward precincts an army of forty thousand men, and served occasionally as a stronghold of the sovereigns against their rebellious subjects. After the kingdom had passed into the hands of the Christians, the Alhambra continued to be a royal demesne, and was occasionally inhabited by the Castilian monarchs. The emperor Charles V commenced a sumptuous palace within its walls, but was deterred from completing it by repeated shocks of earthquakes. The last royal residents were Philip V and his beautiful queen, Elizabetta of Parma, early in the eighteenth century. Great preparations were made for their reception. The palace and gardens were placed in a state of repair, and a new suite of apartments erected, and decorated by artists brought from Italy. The sojourn of the sovereigns was transient, and after their departure the palace once more became desolate. Still the place was maintained with some military state. The governor held it immediately from the crown, its jurisdiction extended down into the suburbs of the city, and was independent of the captain-general of Granada. A considerable garrison was kept up; the governor had his apartments in the front of the old Moorish palace, and never descended into Granada without some military parade. The fortress, in fact, was a little town of itself, having several streets of houses within its walls, together with a Franciscan convent and a parochial church.

The desertion of the court, however, was a fatal blow to the Alhambra. Its beautiful halls became desolate, and some of them fell to ruin; the gardens were destroyed, and the fountains ceased to play. By degrees the dwellings became filled with a loose and lawless population: *contrabandistas*, who availed themselves of its independent jurisdiction to carry on a wide and daring course of smuggling, and thieves and rogues of all sorts, who made this their place of refuge whence they might depredate upon Granada and its vicinity. The strong arm of government at length interfered, the whole community was thoroughly sifted; none were suffered to remain but such as were of honest character, and had legitimate right to a residence; the greater part of the houses were demolished and a mere hamlet left, with the parochial church and the Franciscan convent. During the recent troubles in Spain, when Granada was in the hands of the French, the Alhambra was garrisoned by their troops and the palace was occasionally inhabited by the French commander. With that enlightened taste which has ever distinguished the French nation in their conquests, this monument of Moorish elegance and grandeur was rescued from the absolute ruin and desolation that were overwhelming it. The roofs were repaired, the saloons and galleries protected from the weather, the gardens cultivated, the watercourse restored, and fountains once more made to throw up their sparkling showers; and Spain may thank her invaders for having preserved to her the most beautiful and interesting of her historical monuments.

On the departure of the French they blew up several towers of the outer wall, and left the fortifications scarcely tenable. Since that time the military importance of the post is at an end. The garrison is a handful of invalid soldiers, whose principal duty is to guard some of the outer towers, which serve occasionally as a prison of state; and the governor, abandoning the lofty hill of the Alhambra, resides in the centre of Granada, for the more convenient despatch of his official duties. . . .

Leaving our *posada,* and traversing the renowned square of the Vivar-rambla, once the scene of Moorish jousts and tournaments, now a crowded market-place, we proceeded along the Zacatin, the main street of what, in the time of the Moors, was the Great Bazaar, and where small shops and narrow alleys still retain the Oriental character. Crossing an open place in front of the palace of the captain-general, we ascended a confined and winding street, . . . led up to the Puerta de las Granadas, a massive gateway of Grecian architecture, built by Charles V, forming the entrance to the domains of the Alhambra.

At the gate were two or three ragged super-annuated soldiers, dozing on a stone bench . . . while a tall, meagre varlet, whose rusty-brown cloak was evidently intended to conceal the ragged state of his nether garments, was lounging in the sunshine and gossiping with an ancient sentinel on duty. He joined us as we entered the gate, and offered his services. . . .

I have a traveller's dislike to officious ciceroni, and did not altogether like the garb of the applicant.

"You are well acquainted with the place, I presume?"

"Ninguno mas; pues, señor, soy hijo de la Alhambra." — (Nobody better, in fact, sir, I am a son of the Alhambra!)

The common Spaniards have certainly a most poetical way of expressing themselves. "A son of the Alhambra!" the appellation caught me at once; the very tattered garb of my new acquaintance assumed a dignity in my eyes. It was emblematic of the fortunes of the place, and befitted the progeny of a ruin.

I put some further questions to him, and found that his title was legitimate. His family had lived in the fortress from generation to generation ever since the time of the Conquest. His name was Mateo Ximenes. "Then, perhaps," I said, "you may be a descendant from the great Cardinal Ximenes?" *"Dios Sabe!* God knows, señor! It may be so. We are the oldest family in the Alhambra, — *Christianos viejos,* old Christians. . . . My father knows all about it; he has the coat-of-arms hanging up in his cottage, up in the fortress." There is not any Spaniard, however poor, but has some claim to high pedigree. The first title of this ragged worthy, however, had completely captivated me, so I gladly accepted the services of the "son of the Alhambra."

We now found ourselves in a deep, narrow ravine, filled with beautiful groves, with a steep avenue, and various footpaths winding through it, bordered with stone seats, and ornamented with fountains. To our left we beheld the towers of the Alhambra beetling above us; to our right, on the opposite side of the ravine, we were equally dominated by rival towers on a rocky eminence. These, we were told, were the *torres vermejos,* or vermilion towers, so called from their ruddy hue. No one knows their origin. They are of a date much anterior to the Alhambra: some suppose them to have been built by the Romans; others, by some wandering colony of Phoenicians. Ascending the steep and shady avenue, we arrived at the foot of a huge square Moorish tower, forming a kind of barbican, through which passed the main entrance to the fortress. Within the barbican was another group of veteran invalids, one mounting guard at the portal, while the rest, wrapped in their tattered cloaks, slept on the stone benches. This portal is called the Gate of Justice, from the tribunal held within its porch during the Moslem domination, for the immediate trial of petty causes — a custom common to the Oriental nations, and occasionally alluded to in the sacred Scriptures. "Judges and officers shalt thou make thee *in all thy gates,* and they shall judge the people with just judgment."

The great vestibule, or porch of the gate, is formed by an immense Arabian arch, of the horseshoe form, which springs to half the height of the tower. On the keystone of this arch is engraven a gigantic hand. Within the vestibule, on a keystone of the portal, is sculptured, in like manner, a gigantic key. Those who pretend to some knowledge of Mohammedan symbols affirm that the hand is the emblem of doctrine, the five fingers designating the five principal commandments of the creed of Islam, fasting, pilgrimaging, almsgiving, ablution, and war against infidels. The key, say they, is the emblem of the faith or of power; the key of Daoud, or David, transmitted to the prophet. "And the key of the house of David will I lay upon his shoulder; so he shall open and none shall shut, and he shall shut and none shall open." (Isaiah xxii., 22.) The key we are told was emblazoned on the standard of the

Moslems in opposition to the Christian emblem of the cross, when they subdued Spain or Andalusia. It betokened the conquering power invested in the prophet. . . .

After passing through the barbican, we ascended a narrow lane, winding between walls, and came on an open esplanade within the fortress, called the Plaza de los Algibes, or Place of the Cisterns, from great reservoirs which undermine it, cut in the living rock by the Moors to receive the water brought by conduits from the Darro, for the supply of the fortress. Here, also, is a well of immense depth, furnishing the purest and coldest of water, — another monument of the delicate taste of the Moors, who were indefatigable in their exertions to obtain that element in its crystal purity.

In front of this esplanade is the splendid pile commenced by Charles V, and intended, it is said, to eclipse the residence of the Moorish kings. Much of the Oriental edifice intended for the winter season was demolished to make way for this massive pile. The grand entrance was blocked up, so that the present entrance to the Moorish palace is through a simple and almost humble portal in a corner. With all the massive grandeur and architectural merit of the palace of Charles V, we regarded it as an arrogant intruder, and, passing by it with a feeling almost of scorn, rang at the Moslem portal.

While waiting for admittance, our self-imposed cicerone, Mateo Ximenes, informed us that the royal palace was entrusted to the care of a worthy old maiden dame called Doña Antonia Molina, but who, according to Spanish custom, went by the more neighborly appellation of Tia Antonia (Aunt Antonia), who maintained the Moorish halls and gardens in order and showed them to strangers. While we were talking, the door was opened by a plump little black-eyed Andalusian damsel, whom Mateo addressed as Dolores, but who, from her bright looks and cheerful disposition, evidently merited a merrier name. Mateo informed me in a whisper that she was the niece of Tia Antonia, and I found she was the good fairy who was to conduct us through the enchanted palace. Under her guidance we crossed the threshold, and were at once transported, as if by magic wand, into other times and an Oriental realm, and were treading the scenes of Arabian story. Nothing could be in greater contrast than the unpromising exterior of the pile with the scene now before us. We found ourselves in a vast *patio* or court, one hundred and fifty feet in length, and upwards of eighty feet in breadth, paved with white marble, and decorated at each end with light Moorish peristyles, one of which supported an elegant gallery of fretted architecture. Along the mouldings of the cornices and on various parts of the walls were escutcheons and ciphers, and cufic and Arabic characters in high relief, repeating the pious mottoes of the Moslem monarchs, the builders of the Alhambra, or extolling their grandeur and munificence. Along the centre of the court extended an immense basin or tank (*estanque*), a hundred and twenty-four feet in length, twenty-seven in breadth, and five in depth, receiving its water from two marble vases. Hence it is called the Court of the Alberca (from *al beerkah*, the Arabic for a pond or tank). Great numbers of gold-fish were to be seen gleaming through the waters of the basin, and it was bordered by hedges of roses.

Passing from the Court of the Alberca under a Moorish archway, we entered the renowned Court of Lions. No part of the edifice gives a more complete idea of its original beauty than this, for none has suffered so little from the ravages of time. In the centre stands the fountain famous in song and story. The alabaster basins still shed their diamond drops; the twelve which support them, and give the court its name, still cast forth crystal streams as in the days of Boabdil. The lions, however, are unworthy of their fame, being of miserable sculpture, the work probably of some Christian captive. The court is laid out in flower-beds, instead of its ancient and appropriate pavement of tiles or marble; the alteration, an instance of bad taste, was made by the French when in possession of Granada. Round the four sides of the court are light Arabian arcades of open filigree work, supported by slender pillars of white marble, which it is supposed were originally guilded. The architecture, like that in most parts of the interior of the palace, is characterized by elegance rather than grandeur, bespeaking a delicate and graceful taste, and a disposition to indolent enjoyment. When one looks upon the fairy traces of the peristyles, and the apparently fragile fretwork of the walls, it is difficult to believe that so much has survived the wear and tear of centuries, the shocks of earthquakes, the violence of war, and the quiet, though no less baneful, pilferings of the tasteful traveller; it is almost sufficient to excuse the popular tradition that the whole is protected by a magic charm.

On one side of the court a rich portal opens into the Hall of the Abencerrages: so called from the gallant cavaliers of that illustrious line who were here perfidiously massacred. There are some who doubt the whole story, but our humble cicerone Mateo pointed out the very wicket of the portal through which they were introduced one by one into the Court of Lions, and the white marble fountain in the centre of the hall beside which they were beheaded. He showed us also certain broad ruddy stains on the pavement, traces of their blood, which, according to popular belief, can never be effaced.

Immediately oppose the Hall of the Abencerrages, a portal, richly adorned, leads into a hall of less tragical associations. It is light and lofty, exquisitely graceful in its architecture, paved with white marble, and bears the suggestive name of the Hall of the Two Sisters. Some destroy the romance of the name by attributing it to two enormous slabs of alabaster which lie side by side, and form a great part of the pavement: an opinion strongly supported by Mateo Ximenes. Others are disposed to give the name a more poetical significance, as the vague memorial of Moorish beauties who once graced this hall, which was evidently a part of the royal harem. This opinion I was happy to find entertained by our little bright-eyed guide, Dolores, who pointed to a balcony over an inner porch, which gallery, she had been told, belonged to the women's apartment. "You see, señor," she said, "it is all grated and latticed, like the gallery in a convent chapel where the nuns hear mass; for the Moorish kings," added she, indignantly, "shut up their wives just like nuns."

The latticed "jalousies," in fact, still remain, whence the dark-eyed beauties of the harem might gaze unseen upon the *zambras* and other dances and entertainments of the hall below.

On each side of this hall are recesses or alcoves for ottomans and couches, on which the voluptuous lords of the Alhambra indulged in that dreamy repose so dear to the Orientalists. A cupola or lantern admits a tempered light from above and a free circulation of air; while on one side is heard the refreshing sound of waters from the Fountain of the Lions, and on the other side the soft splash from the basin in the garden of Lindaraxa.

It is impossible to contemplate this scene, so perfectly Oriental, without feeling the early associations of Arabian romance, and almost expecting to see the white arm of some mysterious princess beckoning from the gallery, or some dark eye sparkling through the lattice. The abode of beauty is here as if it had been inhabited but yesterday; but where are the two sisters, where the Zoraydas and Lindaraxas!

An abundant supply of water, brought from the mountains by old Moorish aqueducts, circulates throughout the palace, supplying its baths and fish-pools, sparkling in jets within its halls or murmuring in channels along the marble pavements. When it has paid its tribute to the royal pile, and visited its gardens and parterres, it flows down the long avenue leading to the city, tinkling in rills, gushing in fountains, and maintaining a perpetual verdure in those groves that embower and beautify the whole hill of the Alhambra.

WASHINGTON IRVING
Tales of the Alhambra, 1828

Because he was in the habit of getting there ahead of the avant-garde in all departments of art and life, it is remarkable that the author of Mademoiselle de Maupin *waited until the summer of 1842, when he was a seasoned and well-published thirty-one, to visit the Alhambra. Despite the fact that everybody had already been there, Théophile Gautier found no trouble getting the* Revue des Deux Mondes *to accept the following account, which appeared under the title of "A Summer in Spain."*

We were so passionately fond of the Alhambra that, not satisfied with going there every day, we desired to live there altogether; not in the neighbouring houses, which are rented at very high prices to the English, but within the palace itself; and thanks to the protection of our Granada friends, we were told that, though a formal permission could not be granted to us, our presence there would not be taken notice of. We spent four days and four nights in the palace, and they were unquestionably the most delightful days of my life. . . .

. . . This is assuredly a dwelling where dust will not trouble one, and the wonder is how such rooms could be inhabited in winter. No doubt the great cedar gates were then closed, the marble pavement covered with thick rugs, and fires of fruit-pippins and scented wood lighted in the braseros; and thus the inhabitants awaited the return of the warm season, which is never long delayed in Granada.

We shall not describe the Hall of the Abencerrages, which is very similar to that of the Two Sisters and has nothing remarkable save its old lozenged wooden gate, which goes back to the time of the Moors. In the Alcazar at Seville there is another in exactly the same style.

The Lion Fountain enjoys, in Arab poetry, a marvellous reputation; there is no praise too great for these superb animals. For my part, I am bound to confess that it would be difficult to find anything less like lions than these works of African fancy. The paws are more like those rough pieces of wood that are put into the stomachs of cardboard dogs to preserve their equilibrium; the faces, rayed with cross-bars, no doubt intended to figure the moustaches, are exactly like the mouths of hippopotami; the eyes are of such primitive drawing that they recall the shapeless attempts of children: and yet these twelve monsters, if considered not as lions but as chimeras, as caprices of ornamentation, produce, with the basin which they upbear, a picturesque and elegant effect which enables one to understand their reputation and the praise contained in the Arabic inscription, in twenty-four lines of twenty-two syllables, engraved upon the sides of the basin into which falls the water from the upper basin. It was into this fountain that fell the heads of the thirty-six Abencerrages drawn into the trap by the Zegris. The other Abencerrages would all have suffered the same fate but for the devotion of a little page, who hastened, at the risk of his own life, to warn the survivors and prevent their entering the fatal court. At the bottom of the basin are pointed out great red stains, an indelible accusation left by the victims against their cruel executioners. Unfortunately, learned men pretend that the Abencerrages and the Zegris never existed. On this point I trust wholly to the ballads, the popular traditions, and the novels of Chateaubriand, and I am firmly convinced that the red stains are due to blood. . . .

The Generalife is situated a short distance from the Alhambra upon a hump of the same mountain. It is reached by a sort of hollow road which crosses the los Molinos ravine, bordered with fig trees with enormous shining leaves, green oaks, pistachios, laurels, and rock roses, all growing with incredible richness. The ground on which you walk consists of yellow sand permeated with water and extraordinarily fertile. Nothing is more delightful than this road, which seems to cut through an American virgin forest, so full of flowers and varied is it, so heavy is the perfume of the aromatic plants. Vines grow out of the cracks of the broken-down walls and hang their fanciful tendrils and their leaves, outlined like Arab ornaments, on every branch. The aloe opens out its fan of azure blades, the orange tree twists its knotty trunk and clings to the bricks of the escarpment. Everything blooms and flowers in a thick disorder full of delightful and unexpected happenings. A stray branch of jessamine mingles its white stars with the scarlet flowers of the pomegranate, and a cactus on one side of the road is, in spite of its thorns, embraced by a laurel on the other. Nature, left to herself, seems to become coquettish, and to insist on showing how far behind her is even the most exquisite and consummate art.

It is a fifteen minutes walk to the Generalife, which is a sort of country house of the Alhambra. The exterior, like that of all Eastern buildings, is exceedingly plain: high, windowless walls, surmounted by a terrace, with an arcaded gallery, and over all a small modern look-out. Nothing is left of the Generalife but arcades and great arabesque panels, unfortunately overlaid with whitewash, which is renewed with despairingly obstinate cleanliness. Little by little all the delicate grace, the marvellous modelling of this fairy architecture are vanishing, filling up and disappearing. What is now but a faintly vermiculated wall was formerly a piece of lace as delicate as the sheets of ivory which the patient Chinese carve into fans. The whitewasher's brush has destroyed more masterpieces than the scythe of Time, if we may use this mythological and worn-out comparison. . . .

The real charms of the Generalife are its gardens and its water-works. A marble-lined canal runs the whole length of the enclosure, and its full, rapid stream flows under a succession of arcades of foliage formed by colossal clipped yews; orange trees and cypresses are planted on either bank. At the foot of one of these cypresses, which is of monstrous size and which goes

back to the time of the Moors, Boabdil's favourite, if the legend is to be believed, proved many a time that bolts and bars are but slight guarantees of the virtue of sultanas. What is quite certain is that the yew tree is very large and very old.

The perspective is closed by a galleried portico with jets of water and marble columns like the Patio de los Arrayanes at the Alhambra. The canal turns, forms a loop, and you enter other enclosures adorned with ponds, on the walls of which are the remains of frescoes of the sixteenth century representing rustic buildings and landscapes. In the centre of one of these ponds blooms, like a vast bouquet, a gigantic rose-laurel of incomparable beauty and brilliancy. When I saw it, it looked like an explosion of flowers, like a bouquet of vegetable fireworks, a splendid and vigorous mass of noisy freshness, if such a word may be applied to colours which would cause the most brilliant rose to pale. Its lovely flowers bloomed out with all the ardour of desire towards the pure light of heaven; its noble leaves, designed expressly by nature as a crown for gladiators, were laved by the spray of the jets of water and sparkled like emeralds in the sunshine. Nothing has ever given me such a deep sensation of beauty as that rose laurel in the Generalife.

THÉOPHILE GAUTIER
"A Summer in Spain," 1842

POETS AT THE ALHAMBRA

A year after his prose account of that rose laurel, Gautier published a poem, "Dans le Généralife, il est un laurier-rose. . . ." The circumstances of its first appearance were odd. The poet had just met a deadline with a theater review at La Presse when word reached him from a panicky editor that the printer had lost his copy. Gautier replied that he would sooner saw off his right hand with his left than write the same story twice and submitted the poem instead, with a note telling his readers that he had dashed off the verses while at Granada, "at a time of our life when we didn't have to work on Sundays."

There's a rose laurel in the Generalife
That shines like love or victory in full cry —
Its nurse (a fountain) tenders it relief
In a shower of pearls o'er flower and leaf
Whose cool lustre disdains the fiery sky.

My presence made it blush like a nymphette,
Tingeing its petals with a rosy hue —
And in the mirrored shape beneath, I met
In fancy with a slave at her toilette,
Bending over the water framed in blue.

And not a single flower did I miss,
But dallied with them all, happy and free —
And one like a moist red mouth I'd kiss
Till as I pressed it to my lips (ah bliss!)
I knew the flower-mouth was kissing me . . .

THÉOPHILE GAUTIER
Translated by DAVID RATTRAY
"The Rose Laurel in the Generalife," 1843

Born at Fuentevaqueros in the province of Granada in 1898, Federico García Lorca lived and breathed the spirit of Andalusian Spain and was increasingly drawn into the Islamic side of his heritage. The poet's vision of Granada and its Red Citadel comes through in a gentle light in the following description of the city at daybreak in summertime. It is from Impressions and Landscapes, *his first book, published when he was twenty.*

Far-off mountains ripple on the horizon in a suave reptilian rhythm, and the infinitely crystalline transparency of the sky lends increasing brightness to the mat texture of the landscape. Amid patches of shadow dark as jungles, the city lazily unveils, exposing cupolas and ancient towers illuminated in a soft golden light.

Houses like fat, empty-eyed faces loom up through the greenery, and in the gardens tendrils and tall spires of grass and scarlet poppies sway in a thousand gracious rhythms to the music of a solar wind.

Shadows lengthen in languidly smudged outlines, and the air is full of the sonorous soft flute sounds and ocarina chirping of the birds.

Middle distances float in an indecisive haze of sunflowers and avenues, and on some mornings when the dew is still on the ground, a distant bleating in F major may be heard.

Over the blue and green-stained valley of the Dorro, doves (their black and white markings sharply defined) fly in out of the country and alight in poplar groves or massive beds of yellow flowers.

While heavy churchbells hang still in muffled sleep, a single small goatbell jangles ingenuously, at the foot of a cypress tree next to a gypsy's cave on a flank of the Albaicín.

Reeds and rushes and camel grass bend over the water expectantly, waiting to kiss the sun the moment it is mirrored there. . . .

When the sun comes up, it is without any special splendor. Shadows come and go, and gradually the town is suffused in a light purple hue, while the mountains turn into solid gold, and the treetops take on the resplendency of a Florentine apotheosis.

Then all the soft, mellow patches and indecisive hints of blue transmute into a blaze of luminosity, and the ancient towers of the Alhambra glare redly. . . .

The houses of the surrounding town are of a radiant whiteness now, and the darkest thickets bathe in sunlight, green and gold.

The Andalusian sun starts singing a fire song, and all Creation trembles at the sound.

The light is so magical (and in fact, unique) that birds passing through the air here change into rare and noble metals, pink opals, solid rainbows. . . .

The smoke of the first cooking fires climbs over the town, overspreading it with a ponderous, incensed cloud . . . The sun shines on, and the sky that was so pure and fresh is now a dirty white . . . A mill revives its serenade, held since yesterday sunset in abeyance. Somewhere in the distance, a cock crows at the thought of the bright red sky at dawn. And the mad crickets of the surrounding plain are already tuning up, in anticipation of a perfectly drunken afternoon.

FEDERICO GARCIA LORCA
Impressions and Landscapes, 1918

REFERENCE

Chronology of Islamic Spain

Entries in boldface refer to the Alhambra

A.D. 411   Vandals, a wandering Germanic people, overrun Roman Spain

453   Another Germanic people, the Visigoths, establish a kingdom in Spain that lasts 300 years

570   Birth of the Prophet Muhammad in Mecca

622   Muhammad migrates from Mecca to Medina, beginning Islamic era

632   Death of Muhammad; he is succeeded as caliph by four close associates, the last of whom is his son-in-law Ali

636   Battle of Yarmuk secures Syria for Islam

639   Muslims begin conquest of Egypt

641   Muslims take Persia

661   Muawiya, governor of Syria, seizes caliphate and founds Umayyad dynasty, based in Damascus

705   North Africa is consolidated under Muslim rule

710   First reconnaissance of southern tip of Spain by Muslim Berbers

711   Mixed force of Arabs and Berbers, under Tariq ibn-Ziyad, lands at Gibraltar; within three years Spain becomes a part of the Umayyad empire

714   Muslims cross Pyrenees, raid Gaul

718   Battle of Covadonga; Asturian chief Pelayo checks the Muslim advance in northwest Spain

720   Narbonne falls to the Muslims

721   Muslims are defeated at Toulouse by Duke Eudes of Aquitaine

732   Muslim expansion into Western Europe is checked by victory of Charles Martel near Poitiers

750   Persian-based Abbasids revolt against Umayyads and inaugurate their own dynasty, moving caliphate to Baghdad

756   Abd-al-Rahman ibn-Muawiyah, a surviving Umayyad, reaches Spain and sets up — and over ten years consolidates — an independent emirate

777   Charlemagne invades Spain

778   Charlemagne withdraws to cope with problems at home; his rear guard is badly beaten by Basques in Roncesvalles in the Pyrenees

780–850   Al-Khwarizmi, mathematician, author of treatise on algebra

786   Abd-al-Rahman founds Great Mosque at Cordoba

822–52   Reign of Abd-al-Rahman II, patron of music and astronomy; he attempts to make Cordoba a city that will rival Baghdad

844   Normans begin raids on Spanish coasts

850   Christians begin imitating Arab way of life, attracted by Muslim civilization and amenities

878   Earliest documentary evidence of a citadel on the Alhambra hill

912–61   Reign of Abd-al-Rahman III; Cordoba equals, the splendors of Baghdad and Constantinople

929   Abd-al-Rahman III declares himself caliph of Cordoba, taking title of al-Nasir, "the Victorious"

961–76   Reign of al-Hakam II, founder of the great library of Cordoba, and of the university

976   Dictatorship of the chamberlain Almanzor begins

994–1064   Ibn-Hazm, philosopher and poet, founder of comparative religion

999   Bishop Gerbert elected pope, he reflects Islamic influence

1002   Death of Almanzor; Cordoba caliphate disintegrates with various ineffective Umayyad candidates competing for power.

1021–58   Ibn-Gabirol, Jewish Neoplatonist, author of *Fons Vitae*

1031   Cordoba caliphate collapses, introducing age of *taifa* (faction) kinglets; Andalus breaks up into a score of petty states

1037   The Christian states of Galicia, León, and Castile are briefly united under Ferdinand I; this unity is broken at his death, but León and Castile are temporarily reunited by his son Alfonso VI

1040   Al-Mutamid, the poet-king, accedes to rule of the most important *taifa* state, based in Seville; he wars against Alfonso VI and the Cid

1085   Toledo falls to the Christians, soon becomes great clearinghouse for transmittal of Arabic culture and science to Western Europe

1086   The Almoravide Yusuf ibn-Tashfin, at the request of al-Mutamid and others, crosses into Spain and defeats Alfonso VI at Badajoz, then returns to Morocco to suppress discord at home

1090   Returning from Morocco, ibn-Tashfin deposes al-Mutamid and includes Andalus in new Almoravide empire based in Marrakesh

1094   The Cid seizes Valencia, preventing Almoravide advance up eastern coast of Spain; death of al-Bakri, Cordoban geographer

1099   Death of the Cid

1100–66   Al-Idrisi, greatest medieval geographer

Guide to the Alhambra

The hill of the Alhambra, whose shape has been likened to that of an enormous boat anchored between the mountain and the plain, forms the westernmost spur of the Sierra Nevada mountain range. Its steep slopes, abundantly wooded today, were sparsely planted in Moorish times, thus rendering impossible a stealthy approach to the Alhambra wall. This exceptionally high, red rampart follows the curves and dips of the long hilltop, forming an unbroken defensive enceinte that is strengthened by twenty-three sturdy towers spaced at irregular intervals. The hill is roughly half a mile in length and some 550 feet across at its widest point.

The enclosure formed by the rampart was divided into three parts, following the natural divisions of the hilltop itself, which has one plateau at its western end and another higher plateau at its midsection — after which it slopes off gently in a broad eastern stretch.

The first division — the hilltop's western plateau — was occupied by the **Alcazaba,** a compact citadel that functioned as military headquarters for the Alhambra complex. Into this part of the fortress were crowded government offices, the mint, guards' barracks, and apartments for members of the court and other official residents and guests.

The second division — comprising the highest, central part of the hilltop — was occupied by the **Alhambra Palace** housing the sultan, his harem, and a constant procession of the state's most important official visitors.

Finally, the whole eastern part of the hilltop constituted a royal city with its own shops, workshops, dwelling houses, baths, *madrasa* (a college), and a great mosque. Of all this, apart from the ruins of two houses and the long-buried foundations of a few others, nothing remains. In all probability the houses that have vanished were of simple construction, taking their amenities from shrubs and shade. But bare of external majesty as it might have been, the royal city was all elegance within. This densely populated honeycomb of cool interiors and patios with fountains was predicated upon an artificially created abundance of water. One of the first things the thirteenth-century builders of the Alhambra did was to construct an aqueduct to bring water down the mountain.

A modern visitor wishing to visit the Alhambra from the lower town should start at Plaza Nueva and proceed up the steep Calle de los Comeres through the modern entrance formed by the **Gate of the Granadas,** a sixteenth-century triumphal arch bearing the arms of Charles V and replacing an earlier Moorish gate. Advancing into the park, a cool oasis planted with elms and filled with the sound of running water, the visitor is faced with three diverging routes.

To the left is a footpath leading past a splendid fountain of Charles V up to the Gate of Justice. To the right of the gate, a lower road slopes off toward the entrance to the Court of the Generalife. Above the gate are the **Vermilion Towers,** which occupy the western end of Monte Mauror, a high ridge paralleling the Alhambra to the south. The Vermilion Towers form an older outwork to the Alhambra proper and are connected with it by a wall effectively sealing off its western approaches.

The third route up the Alhambra hill from the Gate of the Granadas is a motor road called the Paseo de la Alhambra. The grand entrance to the Alhambra is the **Gate of Justice.** This gate is so called because the sultans of Granada dispensed judgment there, a Near Eastern custom of immemorial antiquity. Erected in 1348 by Sultan Yusuf abu al-Hajaj, one of the great builders and decorators of the Alhambra, the gate bears an inscription ending with the words: "May the Almighty make this gate a protecting bulwark, and may He write down its construction among the imperishable actions of the just."

Over the arch is an open hand, symbolizing the five requirements of Islam: belief in the oneness of God, prayer, fasting during the month of Ramadan, almsgiving, and pilgrimage to Mecca.

Continuing through a double gate past a guard room and an inscription of Ferdinand and Isabella, one proceeds through a narrow passageway into the open **Place of the Cisterns,** dominated at its west end by the walls of the Alcazaba. Passing through a southern entrance at the Place of the Cisterns, one steps into a courtyard encompassed with seven towers, the largest of which is the **Watchtower** forming the western tip of the Alhambra fortress. The platform surmounting it affords a visitor a panoramic view of Granada and its long, green plain.

Leaving the Alcazaba, one may now cross the Place of the Cisterns to the unfinished **Palace of Charles V,** site of the Alhambra harem that was demolished following a fire in 1524. The present Renaissance structure is a perfect square in ground plan, with a pompous façade of white stone and a two-storied circular inner court large enough for tournaments and bullfights — the use to which it was originally put.

Cutting east between the south wall of the Renaissance palace and the Gate of Justice, one comes out onto the beginning of the portion of the Alhambra hill on which the now-vanished royal city spread southeast from the **Partal Garden** in the shadow of the Alhambra palace walls and the great mosque that stood where **Santa Maria de la Alhambra** now stands. The great Alhambra mosque was built in 1308 by Muhammad III and was described as follows by Granada's fourteenth-century vizir and historian, ibn-al-Khatib: "It is ornamented with mosaic work and exquisite tracery of the most beautiful and intricate patterns, intermixed with silver flowers and graceful arches, supported by innumerable pillars of the finest polished marble." This mosque was in an excellent state of preservation until the first years of the nineteenth century, at which time Napoleonic occupation forces destroyed it completely.

Having seen this much, one may well wish to take a break before plunging into the intricacies of the Moorish palace. Ideal for such a breathing spell is the **Generalife,** summer villa of the Nasrids. It is fifteen minutes distant from the palace, walking down and around the eastern end of the hill along a curving lane of cypress broadening into a straight avenue running next to a long, thin canal with water jets between clipped hedges and a pair of elongated buildings. The **Court of the Generalife** is one of the oldest extant examples of a Moorish garden. Above it stands the Generalife proper, a villa of fountain and running water; above that a raised

garden with fountain-perforated flights of steps ascending to the hilltop mirador called the **Moor's Seat.** There are shady spots here where one can sit for hours gazing down onto the red walls and towers of the Alhambra and over the city beneath them. The surrounding plain beneath the city and the gaunt foothills of the Sierra up to its snowy peaks along the southeastern horizon afford one a prospect in which the huge distance between arctic and subtropical is compressed, from the lichen of the peaks down to the sugarcane and palm trees of the plain. The Generalife ("Garden of the Architect") was reputedly designed and occupied by one of the Alhambra's original architects. Subsequently purchased by Sultan Isma'il Ibn-Faraj

in about 1320, it has been part of the Alhambra ever since. On even the hottest days in July or August, there is shade and the breezes are cool and refreshing up here.

Reentering the Alhambra via the Gate of Justice one enters a narrow gap between the Moorish palace wall and the northeast face of the Charles V palace, a confined, wedge-shaped yard formed by the juxtaposition of the two. Close to their point of intersection one at last steps through into what has been called the most fascinating building in the world: the **Alhambra Palace.**

The entrance gives directly onto the **Court of the Myrtles,** an extremely elongated oblong whose center is occupied by a large pond between two borders of

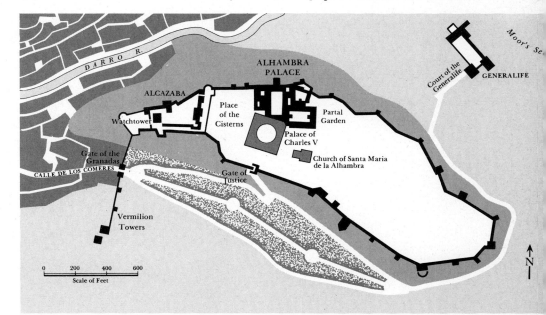

myrtles. To the west of the Court of the Myrtles is the former Meshwar, which housed government offices in Islamic times and was reconstructed as a palace chapel in the sixteenth century. Today it is mostly occupied by gardens.

A colonnaded portico forms the north end of this court and gives onto the ornate **Hall of the Blessing,** an oblong room lying at right angles across the axis of the preceding court, its cedar-wood ceiling a dome of elaborately carved honeycombs and stalactites. Under the Nasrid sultans, the Hall of the Blessing served as anteroom to the throne room, the **Hall of the Ambassadors.** Here, as elsewhere inside the Alhambra, ceilings, beams, and doors are of carved wood; floors and wainscoting are elaborately patterned purple, green and orange mosaics of glazed earthenware; and the remaining ornamental surfaces are of painted stucco, the colors used being the primaries red, blue, and yellow, colors of magic in Sufi tradition. The coloring was laid on with egg white, and it has weathered well, thanks to the dry air of Granada, but the gilding has tarnished to a coppery green in many spots.

Under its sixty-foot-high domed ceiling, the huge square room forming the Hall of the Ambassadors is lit by nine large windows — from which one can look up at the Generalife and the mountainside, or down upon Granada rising in tiers beyond the ravine of the Darro, or simply at the distant mountaintops that edge the horizon. These nine windows are so deeply recessed in the enormous thickness of the walls that they look like the side chapels of a cathedral. "Ill-fated the man who lost all this,"

Charles V exclaimed when he first looked out from here.

The walls to either side are adorned with a pair of laudatory poems by ibn-Zamrak, while exactly between them — in the central recess opposite the entrance — stood the royal throne. Underneath this floor is the center of a complex network of tunnels through which more than one sultan made an eleventh-hour escape. Here too was a dungeon for state prisoners. Situated to the right of the entrance to the Hall of the Ambassadors are the apartments occupied by the newlywed Charles V following his arrival at the Alhambra on June 5, 1526. Three centuries later, the author Washington Irving lived here.

From hence a gallery runs northeast to the **Queen's Dressing Room,** built at the top of a small tower and consisting of a nine-foot-square room. In one cor-

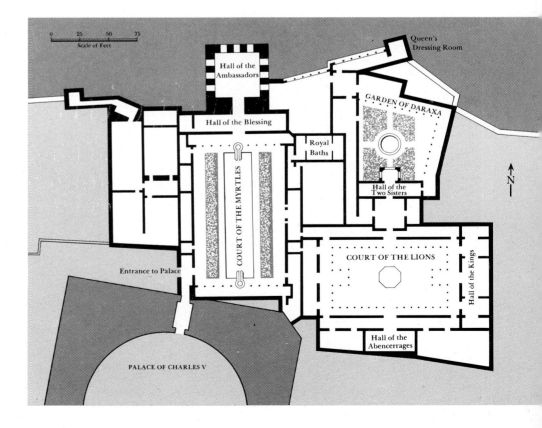

ner is a perforated marble slab through which perfumes were wafted while the queen did her toilette. The walls of the room are covered with paintings of seaports, ships, and naval battles by Italian masters attached to the court of Charles V (and with graffiti scribbled and incised by a dozen generations of courtiers, soldiers, and tourists). A colonnaded porch gives onto a view of the precipitous slopes and defiles of the Albaicin falling headlong at the riverwashed feet of the Alhambra, its sister hill.

From the Albaicin — honeycombed with the famous gypsy cave dwellings which resound to the strains of Flamenco singing and the shrill cries of exuberant, copper-colored children day and night as tourists come and go — the high-perched Plaza de San Nicolas affords the most spectacular overall view of Granada that may be had.

Retracing one's steps from the Queen's Dressing Room to the Hall of the Ambassadors, one enters (via the Hall of the Blessing) a small passageway leading down to the **Royal Baths,** which consist of three large, square rooms. In the entrance room, bathers undressed and then passed on to the steam room, where attendants dashed cold water on them, and from there passed into a chamber of repose, the upper portion of which has a gallery from which musicians performed. Among the inscriptions is the sentence: "What is most to be wondered at is the felicity which awaits in this delightful spot."

Next to the Royal Baths are the **Garden of Daraxa** and its mirador, one of whose chambers is a whispering gallery called the **Hall of Secrets.** Here one hears distinctly from one corner what is being whispered in the opposite corner, thanks to a built-in acoustical feature of the room.

From the mirador of Daraxa one passes into the **Hall of the Two Sisters,** once a part of the private apartments of the Moorish kings, with sleeping alcoves on each side. The Hall of the Two Sisters is so called from two sister slabs of marble embedded in its pavement. The walls are adorned with ibn-Zamrak poems, the calligraphy of which has been called the finest example of cursive epigraphy in Islam.

Through a large door at the south end of the Hall of the Two Sisters one passes into the famous **Court of the Lions.** Enclosed by porticoes and pavilions upheld by more than one hundred irregularly spaced and implausibly slender marble columns, the center of the court is occupied by a fountain consisting of a huge alabaster basin resting on the backs of twelve stone lions of rough, crudely stylized Byzantine mien. A poem is inscribed on the circumference of the basin. The composition of the tile roofs and pavilions balancing the ethereal porticoes around the court is both subtle and strong, while the ornamenting of their interiors has been called a symphony of decoration. "Here," wrote an admiring scholar, "the architecture seems to melt into music." And, added another writer, "Moroccan fantasy here surpasses itself and verges on the Indian. . . ."

Rivaling the Hall of the Two Sisters in the richness and complexity of their ceilings and archways are the **Hall of the Abencerrages** and the **Hall of the Kings,** which face the Court of the Lions from the south and east sides respectively.

The Hall of the Abencerrages is so called from the name of a famous noble family whose male members were reportedly lured there by treachery and executed on orders from Boabdil, last sultan of Granada. (Guides still point out some rusty stains in the floor as "evidence" of this ineffaceable deed.) The ceiling of this hall is lighted by sixteen small windows.

The Hall of the Kings forms the easternmost portion of the Alhambra palace. It received its name from the highly unusual ceiling painting in which ten bearded Moors are reputed to represent the first ten Nasrid rulers. The lacy inner surfaces of the arches in this hall were whitewashed at the orders of Ferdinand and Isabella, who also attended Mass here more than once. Three great windows face east over the **Partal Garden** and the former site of the Alhambra hill's great mosque. Two smaller windows facing into the Court of the Lions give the Hall of the Kings most welcome additional light and limited western exposure as well.

Our nineteenth-century forebears were much addicted to frequenting illustrious monuments by the light of the full moon. Thus illuminated, the Alhambra's halls and courts inspired Chateaubriand, Hugo, Irving, and the generations following them to unexcelled heights of extravagant prose and poetry. Nonetheless, the best light for viewing the inside of the Alhambra is that of the rising or the setting sun, and at both dawn and dusk the silence surrounding the nightingales' singing and the gush and tumble of waters is broken by the clear voice of a bell sounded on the Watchtower and audible on a still day as far as thirty miles away.

Selected Bibliography

Dozy, Reinhart. *Spanish Islam*. London: Chatto & Windus, 1913.

Gibb, Hamilton A.R. *Mohammedanism*. New York: New American Library, 1955.

Glubb, John Bagot. *The Empire of the Arabs*. London: Hodder and Stoughton, 1963.

Hitti, Philip. *History of the Arabs*. New York: St. Martin's Press, 1953.

Irving, Washington. *The Alhambra, Palace of Mystery and Splendor*. New York: Macmillan, 1953.

Levi-Provencal, E. *Histoire de l'Espagne Musulmane* (3 vols.) Paris: Maisonneuve, 1950, 1953.

Nicholson, Reynold A. *A Literary History of the Arabs*. Cambridge: Cambridge University Press, 1953.

Prescott, William H. *History of the Reign of Ferdinand and Isabella*. Carbondale, Ill.: Southern Illinois University Press, 1962.

Stewart, Desmond. *Early Islam*. New York: Time, Inc., 1967.

Watt, W. Montgomery. *A History of Islamic Spain*. Edinburgh: Edinburgh University Press, 1965, (Islamic Surveys Series Number 4).

Wright, Thomas E. *Into the Moorish World*. London: Hale, 1972.

Acknowledgments and Picture Credits

The Editors make grateful acknowledgment for the use of excerpted material from the following works:

"Granada" from *Impresiones y Paisajes* by Federico García Lorca. Copyright © 1964 by the estate of Federico García Lorca. The excerpt appearing on page 160 is published by permission of New Directions Publishing Corporation, agents for the estate.

Into the Moorish World by Thomas E. Wright. Copyright © 1972 by Thomas E. Wright. The excerpt appearing on page 134 is reproduced by permission of Robert Hale & Company.

Jews and Arabs by S. D. Goitein. Copyright © 1955, 1964 by Schocken Books Inc. The excerpt appearing on pages 58–59 is reproduced by permission of Schocken Books Inc.

Sufis of Andalusia. Translated by R. W. J. Austin. Copyright © 1972 by the University of California Press. The excerpts appearing on pages 77 and 79 are reproduced by permission of the regents of the University of California.

The Editors would like to thank Dr. Margaret Clarke in London for her research assistance and David G. Rattray in New York for compiling The Alhambra in Literature, *the guide to the Alhambra, and the chronology of Islamic Spain, as well as for his translations of the prose excerpts from the works of Dr. Johannes Lange, ibn-al-Khatib, and Federico García Lorca. The Editors would also like to express their particular appreciation to Adam Woolfitt in London for his creative photography and to Jane de Cabanyes in Madrid for her art research. In addition, the Editors would like to thank the following individuals and organizations:*

The American Numismatic Society — Michael L. Bates

Lynne Anderson, Los Angeles

Russell Ash, London

Biblioteca Nacional, Madrid — Don Ramón Paz

Dr. Norman Daniel, Cairo

Hispanic Society of America — Dorothy Ann Kostuch

Dr. Maan Z. Madina, New York

Barbara Nagelsmith, Paris

Don Juan Antonio F. Oronoz, Madrid

Lynn Seiffer, New York

Spanish National Tourist Office — Carlos Sánchez Pachón

The title or description of each picture appears after the page number (boldface), followed by its location. Photographic credits appear in parenthesis. The following abbreviations are used:

BN, P — Bibliothèque Nacionale, Paris

MAN — Museo Arqueológico Nacional, Madrid

(O) — Don Juan Antonio F. Oronoz

(AW) — Adam Woolfitt

ENDPAPERS Wooden ceiling in the Hall of the Blessing, Alhambra. (AW) HALF TITLE Symbol by Jay J. Smith Studio FRONTISPIECE Royal Baths, Alhambra. (AW) **9** The Alhambra Vase, 14th century. Museo de Alhambra, Granada (O) **10–11** The Queen's Dressing Room and Comares Tower. (AW) **12** Page from the Koran, Granada, 1304. BN, P, Ms. Arabe, 385, fol 123.

117 Woodcut of a Spanish galleon, from Christopher Columbus's *Letter to Sanchez*, Basel, 1493. Both pages 116–17 Astor, Lenox & Tilden Foundations, New York Public Library **119** The Alhambra from the Moor's Seat. (AW) **120** Engraving of the Spanish Inquisition, from Van Limborch's *Historia Inquisitionis*, 1692. British Museum **122–23** Felipe Vigarny's relief of the baptism of the Moors, from the Royal Chapel, Granada, 1522. Catedral de Granada (O)

CHAPTER VII **125** Alhambra tilework. (AW) **126–27** top, Southeast corner of the Court of the Myrtles, Alhambra. (AW); bottom, The Royal Baths, Alhambra (O) **127** Patio of the Meshwar, Alhambra. (AW) **129** View from the doorway of the mihrab, Alhambra. (AW) **130** Limestone medallions of Charles V and Isabel of Portugal, *c.* 1535–40. Hispanic Society of America **130–31** Interior courtyard of Palace of Charles V, Alhambra. (AW) **132–33** Gardens and fountains of the Generalife, Alhambra. All: (AW) **135** Lions from the fountain in the Court of the Lions, Alhambra. (AW)

THE ALHAMBRA IN LITERATURE **136** Page from the Beato of San Sever, *Commentary on the Apocalypse*, 11th century. BN, P Ms. Lat. 8878, fol. 1 **138–60** Twenty-one illustrations from Girault de Prangey's *Souvenirs de Granada et de l'Alhambra. . .* , Paris, 1837. New York Public Library

REFERENCE **165–66** Maps by Francis & Shaw, Inc.

Index